John, Paul & Me:

Before The Beatles

Len Garry

John, Paul & Me
by Len Garry
First Edition
© 1997 CG Publishing Ltd London
© 1997 CG Publishing Inc Toronto
ISBN 0-9695736-8-5
Manufactured in Canada
Pictured opposite: Pete Shotton, Billy Turner, John Lennon, Len Garry
Cover Photo Paul McCartney, Len Garry, John Lennon - November 23rd 1957 Clubmoor Hall Liverpool
Editor - Robert Godwin
Cover design by Gene Quandamatteo

John, Paul & Me

Len Garry

This book is dedicated to my dear wife Susan and to my four children
Robert, Jonathan, Ruth and Jane.
I would especially like to mention the following:
Jenny Manger for deciphering my hand-writing and typing up the manuscript.
Pete Shotton for his valuable contribution and renewed friendship.
The 'gang' - John Lennon, Pete Shotton, Nigel Whalley, Ivan Vaughan and Billy Turner
And to the other original members of the Quarrymen skiffle group, Sir Paul McCartney, Rod
Davis, Colin Hanton and Eric Griffiths.

Introduction

I had no intention of writing yet "another book" about the Beatles. I was convinced that people - even fanatic Beatles fans - were bored to death by now at the amazing number of Beatles books that had been written. It had always amazed me that most of these books had been written by people who had no first hand account of what it was like at the start of things. This book came about after a chance meeting at the 1995 Beatles convention in Liverpool to which I, my wife and two daughters regularly attend.

One evening, during the convention, my wife Susan and I had arranged to meet Mike Wilshaw (the guy who wrote the hit song Juliet), in the Adelphi foyer. Just by chance a certain gentleman passing through the foyer heard that Len Garry - an original "Quarryman" was in the building. This gentlemans name was Chris Tassone from Toronto Canada, who was making a living at the time impersonating Ringo Starr, as well as being a record producer/ promoter and of course an avid Beatles fan. We were introduced and a friendship was formed immediately. Chris then introduced me to another Beatles fanatic called Gene Quondamatteo, also from Canada and we all eventually formed a firm friendship.

Two months later I injured my calf muscle as a consequence of playing basket ball in the course of my present occupation (taking people with learning disabilities for sports sessions, music sessions and summer activities). This meant I was "laid up" for five weeks with nothing to do but rest my leg, and the thought of just lying there watching television did not have great appeal to me at the time.

Then thoughts about writing started to fill my mind. Why don't I write down a few words about my early association with Lennon and McCartney? So I started writing. I eventually informed Gene, who had returned to Canada by this time, of what I had written and he encouraged me to send him the story so far. He rang me soon afterwards and showed such enthusiasm for the manuscript's potential that I carried on. Without his constant support and help I doubt if I would have completed the project.

The book attempts to give a first hand account of the birth and the very early stages in the formation of the most amazing musical phenomenon of this century - THE BEATLES. This is not just a book of facts - it is, however, about friendship and the early bonding of a group of teenagers who were initially brought together on the basis of humour and an incurable sense of fun. I have added dialogue to the facts in order to create atmosphere and convey to the reader what it was really like at the beginning. If I have managed to paint a picture using words so that the reader experiences a sense of "being there" amongst all the mischief making and the first stumbling steps of the "Band that made it really big " (to quote John Lennon's own words), then I will feel I have done something worthwhile.

I hope you enjoy the book.

Len Garry 1997.

THE LIVERPOOL INSTITUTE HIGH SCHOOL,

Lower School.

April 1956.

Paul McCartney

Neil Aspinall

'Duff' Lowe

Len Garry

Contents

One   John And Paul's First Gig Together   **8**

Two   My Early Life   **29**

Three   Meeting John Lennon And The Gang   **43**

Four   Musical Influences On The Quarrymen   **79**

Five   Life Up To The Formation Of The Quarrymen   **94**

            Pete Shotton, John Lennon And The Tea Chest Bass   **112**

            The Jammy Hartley Incident   **132**

            St Peter's Church Garden Fête   **144**

            Wilson Hall John and Paul's Second Gig Together   **170**

Six   A Near Fatal Illness And The Emergence Of The Beatles   **188**

Seven   Epilogue - The Quarrymen Now   **201**

1

John and Paul's First Gig Together:

Saturday 12th of October 1957:

Early this particular Saturday afternoon on a small council estate in the quiet suburb of Allerton in South Liverpool, a group of teenage friends had arranged to meet. The meeting place's official address was No.20 Forthlin Road, Liverpool, 18. It was the home of Jim McCartney and his two young sons; Paul McCartney and his younger brother Michael.

It was a small unassuming residence, identical in appearance to the rest of the small terraced row of properties. It had a small front garden surrounded by a low wall against which were leaning two or three drop handled bicycles, parked in a rather haphazard manner. As one entered the house from the road, after passing along a narrow path that skirted the right hand side of the small garden, one entered from the front door directly into a small circulation area. From this area arose a steep flight of stairs leading up to the first floor. Turning directly left one entered the front sitting room that spanned virtually the whole width of the property. On entering the front room, directly facing you was an old upright piano. Immediately to the right was a fairly modern tiled fireplace. Either side of the fireplace were two armchairs and there was a three seater settee placed under the lounge's "picture style" window. The friends gathered were all the members of the Quarrymen Skiffle group, namely; John Lennon, Len Garry, Nigel Whalley and Eric Griffiths.

Their main objective for the meeting was to discuss and practice for the forthcoming performance of the group that had been arranged for Friday the 18th of October at the New Conservative Club, Clubmoor. The young friends were all lounging about in the front room. Paul McCartney meanwhile was busy in the kitchen. The line up for the Quarrymen had undergone a few changes since the fairly recent performance that had been held at St Peters Church village fête a few months earlier - 6th July to be exact. Pete Shotton who had been the washboard player was no longer in: he had undergone a harrowing experience at the Rosebery Street venue (just before the St Peters show) when John Lennon smashed the washboard over his head and although Pete turned up for the St Peter's performance with a new one he soon after decided to "hang up his washboard". Another departure was Rod Davies who had been the banjo player. He had decided to concentrate more on his school studies instead.

It was about 2:15 p.m. and Paul McCartney was still in the kitchen - he had been there for about 15 minutes making toast for his friends. John Lennon was slouched over an armchair with his legs perched over the side strumming away on his guitar. Len Garry and Nigel Whalley were discussing ways to get to Clubmoor and Eric Griffiths was falling asleep on the settee.

- *"Yeah yeah - it's all very well Paul,"* muttered John Lennon, *"just because your Dad played in some old time music hall in the thirties, doesn't mean we should go on stage wearing white coats. People will think we're a bunch of fairies."* (Fairies being a term for someone effeminate).

- *"Wait a minute John, I'm burning the toast."* Paul, clattering about in the kitchen seemed oblivious to John's emphatic statement. Paul then came out of the kitchen with a pile of buttered toast on a large plate for the ravenous horde waiting.

- *"What did you say? I couldn't hear you properly; oh the white coats, is that what you're on about? What's your problem with that? Look John, it's about time we started smartening up our image because we can't go on looking like a gang of ruffians just dragged off the streets,"* retorted Paul. *"We must look professional - we are on the stage - in the public eye and appearances are important. If we start looking the part then perhaps you may even be able to get your chords right."*

Paul said this last point in a jovial manner, not wishing to rouse John's temper, as he knew even after their short acquaintance with John that he could soon "fly off the handle" if provoked. John seemed unperturbed by the insinuation that Paul was making about his professionalism (or lack of it more to the point).

There was a silence for a couple of minutes as they all munched their buttered toast.

- *"Yeah okay - but white coats? I can't see myself in one of those. Anyway where would we get them from?"*

- *"Never mind that - Nigel will sort that out. Look, it will be you and me up front from now on as main guitarists and vocalists so it will look good the both of us wearing the same gear - it will be white coats, white shirts and black bow ties - the rest of the group can wear white shirts and black bow ties."*

John still seemed undecided and looked to me for support. *"What do you think*

Len?" He asked.

- *"I think the answer lies in the soil"* I said, trying to bring a bit of humour into what seemed to me a contest building up between two strong personalities, each having been used to getting their own way. *"But then again I think that you two don't need us anymore, we're has-beens."* I said, continuing in a none serious vein.

There was however an element of truth in my reply. I was thinking that as the tea chest bass player my instrument was starting to look out of place - as a "home made" instrument and that my playing days were numbered. Things were changing quite quickly. The song repertoire included more Rock 'n' Roll songs now that Paul had become a firm fixture in "the group". We never called ourselves a band, it was always "the group". So much so that it became a standard joke if we happened to see anyone who we were impressed with we would all, almost as a chorus, say: *"Let's have him in the group!"*

- *"Come on Len, be serious for a minute. What do you think?"* Repeated John, who was by this time desperate for support.

- *"I honestly think it's worth a try and it will probably improve our image."* I said half heartedly.

Suddenly John resorted to his lighter mode. *"Ooh Eh! We will look smart - why don't we hire a limousine and dress up as undertakers instead "* He quipped.

- *"Don't be thick John, we'd all have to wear black for that,"* Eric Griffiths suddenly interjected.
- *"Okay we'll all be in white then - it's agreed."* said Paul. John then started up a song that had recently been popularised. *"A white sports coat and a pink carnation. I'm getting dressed up for a dance."* With that John did a little dance around the room. The Quarrymen Committee had arrived at another major decision without too much rancour.

- *"It's a long way out to Clubmoor isn't it?"* asked Eric Griffiths who had been quite quiet but was obviously now thinking of how as a group we would get to the New Clubmoor Hall. This venue was one of many owned by Charlie McBain who also owned and ran Wilson Hall in Garston.

- *"It would be handier if we were playing at Wilson Hall."* I said, as it was only a 10 minute bus ride from Forthlin Road.

In order to travel to Clubmoor we would have to get at least two buses and the thought of hiking and struggling to get the tea chest bass on and off the bus (twice) on the outward journey was not filling me with wonderful thoughts.

It was not the first time that the Quarrymen had smartened up their image. The manager and friend of the group, Nigel Whalley, had taken up a post as an assistant professional at Lee Park Golf Club in South Liverpool. Nigel had been advised by his doctor to take up an outdoor, open air post for his health, as he had for a long time suffered from asthma. Nigel arranged for all the Quarrymen to play for a short gig at the dance to be held there and it was agreed that we should all wear large check shirts with white tassels (Country and Western style). For this particular engagement a friend called John "Duff" Lowe stood in as pianist as we all knew there was a piano available on stage (At that time we were impressed by such performers as Jerry Lee Lewis and Little Richard who were Rock 'n Roll singers / pianists. We would try anything in those days). Nigel had obviously been concerned that if he was responsible and claimed to be the manager of the Quarrymen that his "lads" must make a good impression appearance wise.

- *"Paul,"* I said. *"It's all very well, but where are we going to get the bow ties from - you know we haven't got the money to buy that sort of gear. A white shirt is okay, I've got that and black trousers, I can wear my best school trousers. Anyway they'll have to do! I can't wrangle any cash from my Mum and Dad."*

Everyone agreed that they could not really afford it or see themselves asking their parents for any monetary support — times were pretty hard. After much further discussion and merriment it was finally agreed that Nigel Whalley would be able to get bow ties and even a couple of white jackets from the Golf Club where he worked as assistant professional. Nobody asked him about the details we just left it to our "manager," as we naively thought. "manager" meant that any minor problems like this would be solved by him. Sure enough he succeeded on this occasion.

We were still trying to extract every bit of fun we could out of the decision for Paul and John to wear white coats. *"Here's the men from the funny farm,"* somebody remarked. (Funny farm meaning slang for lunatic asylum and if someone had gone mad they would expect the men in the white coats to come and take them away).

- *"I know,"* said John, *"we could all wear pink carnations and Nigel can stand in the crowd and on a certain signal let's say a wave from me and Nige can throw confetti over us from the crowd."*

We all fell apart. John by this time was uncontrollable and had fallen off the couch and was kicking his feet up in the air in a fit of laughter. This was a way of letting Paul know that although it was his idea that our outfit would be changed - John was taking the sting and the attention away from him by taking the piss out of the decision as much as possible. Saying to Paul in a subtle way, *"Look it's your first time on stage with the Quarrymen - we have been together as a group for a while now, don't overstep the mark."* Paul was already exerting his influence on the group and he hadn't even performed with us yet. I suppose we would have gone on stage still wearing any old thing and none of us really liked the thought of the outfit particularly, as it was, more than likely, there would be Teddy Boy gangs in the audience, who were bound to take the piss and we would be prime targets dressed up like that.

Paul may have got the idea from his father Jim, as he had played in a band in the 1930s and it was really a pre-war uniform.

Saturday 12th October 1957 - Practice session

- *"Let's go through the song list."* said Paul.

He was more of a perfectionist where as Lennon was more spontaneous, with an *"It'll be alright on the night,"* sort of attitude.

- *"Okay,"* said John, *"who's got it? "*

- *"John, we had this written out well over a week ago, remember?"* I said. *"It was on a piece of paper taken out of your English homework exercise book."*

- *"Oh yeah - here it is,"* said John, reaching into his jacket pocket and producing a rough piece of paper with a list of about 18 songs scribbled out. John reached for his glasses and stood up as though he were giving an after dinner speech. In his monotone voice he said:

- *"Ladies and gentleman.....we have compiled a repertoire of melodies tailor made for you, some old songs, some new, some buttered, some blue."*

We all doubled up screaming with laughter and ended up on the floor rolling about. Victor Sylvester -a dance band leader who was very popular at the time was always a target for impersonation; "slow slow, quick, quick, slow," and John commenced to demonstrate a slow fox trot dance. This, in essence, was the type of attitude we all had towards our music making. It was all just very good fun. If we could not have had fun we would not have carried on as a band or as friends. Humour and clowning ran through our rehearsals and to a lesser degree, in our performances.

On the song list were tunes that McCartney could play such as "Twenty Flight Rock," by Eddie Cochrane, "Be Bopa Lula" by Gene Vincent and some stand-by skiffle numbers such as Railroad Bill and Lost John. It was the first time Lennon and McCartney were to be on stage together. Paul's guitar, if my memory serves me right, was called a "Zenith" cello guitar. Eric Griffith's instrument had not changed and his guitar was very similar to that of Paul's.

We went through the song list and after much more merriment and piss-taking impersonations we finished our repertoire and persuaded Paul to re-write the list out properly and Paul being a perfectionist also put the keys of each song in the margin. Where as Lennon would have kept them in his mind, Paul wrote it all down, we were "getting organised." Paul was going to attempt to play a guitar solo called "Guitar Boogie" at this particular performance, which I thought at the time was a particularity bold thing to do, bearing in mind that we were all "unplugged": no amplification, electrification, no sound monitoring. However, Paul brushed all our doubts aside with his confident manner.

- *"Look fellahs, I know this will really add some variety to our usual numbers."* Paul said convincingly and we all finally conceded, bowing to our new lead guitarists authority.

In the music scene at that time there seemed to be quite an influence of instrumental music - such numbers as "Raunchy" were extremely popular. My thoughts varied from that of a tinge of jealousy to those of resignation. Knowing that John was now going to have someone alongside him who was able to give him good vocal support and also introduce harmony (I was previously really the only vocal support to John).

Our musical instruments had not changed much. John still had the same guitar that he played at St Peter's Village fete. Paul's guitar looked so much more classy. I thought at the time it was larger than John's and seemed far better quality (which it was). Although Paul was a left handed guitarist and he had strung it for a left handed player the plectrum guard was still fixed above the 6th string as there was no easy way it could be fitted below, so Paul left it as it was. There is a theory that Paul didn't know how to restring a guitar (for a left-handed player). This has no substance as it would have been impossible for a left handed guitarist to play a right-hand strung guitar. Paul's guitar had that quality and depth of sound and so our actual tonal quality had changed as a group. My instrument, the tea chest bass was still the same, but now on the front, instead of having the white treble clefs on a black background, I had the "Quarrymen" in white capital letters painted on the front, in order to help publicize the name of the group. Colin Hanton had his same set of drums, with his name and that of the "Quarrymen" painted on the bass drum.

- *"What bus do we get to Clubmoor?"* asked Eric.

- *"I think we'll have to get the 81."* I replied.

- *"It'll mean at least two buses."* said Paul.

- *"The 81 goes from Woolton village up the Drive, (Queen's Drive) and then you will have to get the 15D to Broadway."* said Nigel, who had obviously planned the route.

- *"The best thing is that we all meet at the 81 bus stop in the village about 7 p.m.."* said Nigel.

- *"Where's the tea chest now?"* I asked.

- *"It's okay it's at my place."* answered Nigel.

The time was nearing 5 p.m. so we all said our farewells, and jumped on our bikes to go to our respective homes for tea. I arrived back at 77 Lance Lane at about 5.30.

- *"Where have you been son? You haven't been out with that Billy Turner have you?"* asked my mother.

- *"Nah - finished seeing him ages ago Mum. I've been rehearsing with the group. We're playing next week at the Broadway Conservative Club."*

- *"Len, please be careful you hear a lot of stories of lads being beaten up these days. You should spend more time at home. I never seem to see you and you're not eating proper meals. You're so thin."*

- *"It's okay Mum I've had some chips at Paul's place but what's for tea any-way?"* (If I had said I just had toast it would have worried my Mum even more).

- *"Your father's just gone to work ."* said Mum. *"But we've managed to save you some tea."* (Dad had changed to working nights so that he would earn more money).

- *"Ah Mum that's great."* I said giving her a big hug; I loved my Mum greatly and always showed my affection to her.

Tea meant a proper meal, (not just sandwiches), because Dad was working nights we usually ate before 4.30. Tonight it was one of my favourites; liver and onions with white fluffy potatoes and black gravy, finished off with a piece of lemon meringue pie.

- *"Listen Len, you know I'm not one to spoil you having fun but this group you are in - what's it called - a skiffle group? What is it all about?"* asked my Mum, she was rather worried that her son only seemed to eat sporadically and seemed to her to be getting even thinner.

- *"Oh, it's okay Mum, they're a great bunch of kids and don't worry, Billy Turner is not in the group."* Billy Turner was a boy I was banned from seeing.

- *"Just keep clear of trouble Len, because we hear about these Teddy Boy gangs who roam the streets, especially in the Dingle area and they have knuckle-dusters and bicycle chains - why only the other week Mrs Evans' lad got set on by a bunch of hooligans and it was only because the policeman was on his rounds that "E go" Evans (as he was called) was saved from further punish-ment."*

- *"Listen Mum, we'll be alright. Anyway the show is next week and it's at the Conservative Club, you know full well that the Conservatives are snobs and won't cause any trouble."* I said, trying to put my worried mother at ease but knowing all the time that Clubmoor was not a particularly good area of Liverpool, in spite of being called a Conservative Club.

I wolfed my tea down hungrily. I couldn't help being concerned for my moth-er, who I loved very much. I looked at her hands which seemed to be wrinkled far beyond her age of 48 as she sat knitting in the armchair.

- *"Mum I'm not going out tonight. Why don't we both go to the pictures? You don't seem to go out much now that Dad is working nights. I think there is a good Western on at the Gaumont Allerton."*

- *"That's very kind of you Len but the weather has turned quite cold and I don't really feel like walking all that way. I think I'll listen to Saturday night theatre on the radio."*

- *"Okay Mum we'll stay in and listen to it together - I hope it's a murder mys-tery."*

I finished my dinner and took the plate into the kitchen to wash it.

- *"Mum haven't we got any hot water? I'm trying to wash the dishes but the water is only luke warm."*

- *"Ever since your Dad had that new back boiler fitted we can't seem to get any hot water. Your Dad thinks the plumber has put the boiler in wrong and he's going to take him to court for shoddy workmanship."*

- *"There's always something to sort out isn't there Mum? It's going to cost Dad if he loses the case."*

- *"I know. I get worried about your father because he's also trying to sort out your grandmother's estate."*

My Mum's mother had recently died and there was a lot of disputing amongst relatives about the will that grandmother had left. I looked at the mantlepiece where the clock was situated - a clock with a mahogany case given to us by my mother's father before he died. The time was getting near 7.30 p.m. I looked at the small coal fire burning in the cast iron gate, "It will go out if it's not raked properly," I thought and reached for the poker. My father and I had recently replaced the fireplace surround with a more modern tiled one.

- *"I've already given it a good rake Len. I think the ashes need removing from underneath."*

- *"Okay Mum I'll do it."* I removed the cast iron tool from the stand where all the implements for keeping the fire in good working order were hanging. The ash pan was overflowing with smouldering ash. *"I'll get some coal at the same time Mum. We'll have a nice roaring fire in no time. Have we got any chestnuts left?"*

- *"Yes there's some under the stairs,"* said Mum.

I stocked up on coal, replaced the ash pan, drew up my armchair and we both settled down for a quiet evening together. The play on the radio did not start until 9.15 and so we chatted for a little while.

- *"Tell me more about this group you are in. I don't think I've met most of your friends, what are they like?"*

- *"You've met Pete Shotton and John Lennon but I don't think you've met Paul yet."*

- *"Pete is the very tall boy with almost white curly hair isn't he? Yes, I remember him when he called for you a couple of weeks ago - he's the one who rings up as well isn't he?"*

- *"Yes that's him. I think he's the only one who can remember our phone number, Childwall 2936. Well Pete's no longer in the group, we have another lad in now, his name is Paul McCartney."*

I reached for the coal bucket as the fire was getting low and I was becoming bored with all these questions being asked about my friends.

- *"Where is that other lad, you know, the one with the twinkle in his eye and the wavy hair?"*

- *"Oh you mean John - John Lennon. He's still in the group, in fact he's the leader and always has been. Don't you remember you invited him in for tea one Saturday afternoon after we had all been to the Abbey Cinema."*

- *"Oh I remember. They were such polite, well mannered boys."*

- *"You know I only choose the best mates Mum."*

In fact my mother had met the likes of Ivan Vaughan, Pete Shotton, and John Lennon amongst my mates but she was still to meet Paul McCartney. Looking back I can understand her concern. It was unusual for anyone to have friends that lived so far away, but I'd grown apart from the friends of my early years: the ones that lived "just around the corner" because they had no love of popular music.

I looked at the clock, it was now nearly 9:00. In spite of the now roaring fire we still had to huddle around to keep warm. The wind was quite strong that evening and it was lifting the linoleum up off the living room floor: this was because it was blowing through the air vents underneath the wooden joists. My father used to say to me what a benefit this was to the construction of the house as it helped to keep dry rot at bay. I did not know what he was talking about at the time but I pretended I did and agreed with him just to keep him happy.

It was 9:15 and the play was about to start on the radio.

- *"Let's put the lights out and put a few chestnuts around the fire."* I said. Mum agreed.

The remainder of the evening was spent in virtual silence as we toasted our feet before the fire, cracking open chestnuts (which were mostly overcooked) and listened to the murder mystery on the crackling radio.

On Monday 14th October I was back at the Liverpool Institute to continue my studies. I was 15 years old and in the midst of preparing for the preliminary tests in January which determined which subjects you could take the following June 1958 for the General Certificate of Education. The week passed very slowly but eventually Friday evening arrived.

Friday 18th October 1957

It was 4 p.m. and I had just finished school. I arrived home at 4:45 p.m., having had to wait a long time before I could catch a bus that had room on board.

- *"Hi Mum - it's only me."* I shouted through to the kitchen as I entered my home, 77 Lance Lane. You know I'm out tonight don't you?"

- *"Yes I do remember what you tell me Len. Do you want your tea now?"*

- *"No not just yet. I've got to sort out some clothes to wear for the show tonight."*

I had arranged to meet the other members of the group at Woolton Village having arranged to collect the tea chest bass from Nigel Whalley's house before trundling to the 81 bus stop.

- *"Where's my yellow socks Mum? And I'll need my black school trousers, the ones you recently took in at the bottom."* (Mum had recently reduced the width of the trousers from 22" to 16" to make a tighter fit around the ankles).

- *"I've put them in your bottom drawer, where I always put them. Look Len,"* she said impatiently *"I've got Mrs Thomas coming around at 7 o'clock to have her hair done and I've got to clean the place up a bit. Can't you sort yourself out? I'm putting your tea on the table. Don't blame me if it gets cold."*

I shot downstairs and tucked into my evening meal of steak and kidney pie with mashed potatoes, finished off with rice pudding. I felt better: fortified, ready for the evening ahead.

Mum was still having to take in clients to have their hair done, even though Dad was earning more money on the night shift as a compositor on the Liverpool Daily Post and Echo - the local paper. After washing up the dishes I went upstairs to my bedroom to sort out what I was going to wear that evening. I found a neatly ironed white shirt and my luminous yellow socks from the bottom drawer where Mum had said they would be and eventually discovered that my black trousers were hanging in the airing cupboard. I thought that I had better wear my black trousers because I didn't like the idea of having to change in some dingy back room at Clubmoor Hall. I was a shy boy really and was aware that my legs were on the thin side and always felt self conscious. So much so that I often wore two pairs of trousers to try to make my legs look fatter.

I left the outfit all laid out neatly on the bed in the 7'6" by 6'6" bedroom that fronted on to Lance Lane. I looked out of the window at the now denuded cherry blossom that the corporation had planted a couple of years ago. It was a clear, crisp, cold night. John Lennon would probably be in his bedroom, similarly situated at Mendips, sorting out his gear I thought. Something else we had in common. I went back downstairs.

- *"Mum, thanks for tea, it was great - you make a good pie. Will you be alright tonight on your own?"* I was always concerned about leaving my Mum on her own. *"Where's Wal anyway?"* I asked, enquiring about my elder brother Walter.

Mum was as usual in the living room knitting.

- *"Don't mention him,"* she said, *"you should see the types he's knocking around with now."*

I could see that she was getting upset as she talked about her elder son. He was always getting involved in what seemed to us to be very unusual activities, such as yoga and judo. On a number of occasions Wal, being 18 years of age, would just leave home for a few days and not tell anyone where he was going and then suddenly arrive on the doorstep days later with no apology or explanation. This was a cause of great concern for my mother.

- *"Mum I won't go out tonight if you don't feel very well."* I said with anxious concern.
- *"You go on son. I'll be alright."* She said unselfishly. *"Just as long as you're back for 11:30. Leave the front door key under the brick outside the front door just in case. Don't worry about me, just make sure you steer clear of trouble and come home safely, that's all I ask..."*

With that I went up to my bedroom and put on the tight black trousers, making sure that the luminous yellow socks I put on were showing a good splash of yellow. I folded the clean white shirt into a plastic bag ready to put in the bag that was fixed to the back of my Raleigh Rudge bicycle. I put on my gaberdine jacket with the fur collar and collected my bicycle from the garage. The garage at no.77 had only recently been built and it housed a lawn mower, ladders and tools, together with my bicycle and that of my brother Walter. As yet there was no car because my father could not afford one at the time.

It was dark by now and quite cold as I wheeled my bicycle out of the garage. I checked that the dynamo was working properly (this ran off the back wheel and provided lighting, front and back). It had the unfortunate effect of slowing down the speed in order to generate power by pressing on the rear tyre. It also made a strange whirring sound as it generated the electricity. The lights were essential, I did not want to get caught by the local policeman who might happen to be on his rounds that evening. Also the journey to Woolton along the leafy, dark suburbs of South Liverpool was not particularly well lit. There was another hazard, although the city of Liverpool had decided to abolish the tramcars that ran on steel tramlines set in the main roads, the tramlines themselves had not yet been taken up and it could lead to a nasty accident if my front wheel got caught in one.

Because of the cold I searched for the glove which I sometimes wore when playing the tea chest (this was worn on my left hand to prevent me getting bad blisters brought about by the constant tightening of the string against the broom handle in order to vary the notes). I found it in my saddle bag, it would give me some protection, I thought as I set off.

It was about half an hour's ride to Woolton and the time as I looked at my watch was 6:30 p.m. At least it's dry I thought as I rode along Dudlow Lane that evening and wondered what the scene would be like at Paul's house in Forthlin Road and at John Lennon's in Mendips. I could imagine that almost similar questions had been asked by the parents of the boys involved. Jim McCartney would be asking Paul about this new group he was about to make his debut with and would be giving him advice about how to be careful and come home at a reasonable hour and so forth. However I didn't dwell on what Paul would be doing as I turned into Menlove Avenue and I began to whistle the tune "Moonlight Bay," the theme song from Doris Day's film. It wasn't the song I was particularly fond of, it was because it brought me a certain sense of comfort, a feeling of safety and well-being some how. Rock 'n' Roll songs to me conveyed a feeling of danger and excitement and at the moment I needed something soothing and relaxing.

Meanwhile John Lennon was having a heated discussion with his Aunt Mimi at Mendips.

- *"John!"* Mimi shouts up to John's bedroom (which was the small 11' by 7' bay windowed room over the front porch).

- *"John!"* She shouts even harder to try to make her rather timid voice heard over the rather loud music that was blaring out from the bedroom. *"John, are you out tonight? That girl Barbara has been around here earlier asking for you."*

— Barbara Baker - John's girl friend —

Barbara Baker was John's girlfriend who he had been going out with for over a year. John Lennon actually opened the bedroom door, although somewhat reluctantly, as he was preparing himself for the evening's performance in Clubmoor. Earlier he had been wondering what it was going to be like playing for the first time with his newly found friend Paul McCartney.

- *"Look Auntie, if she calls again can you tell her I'll see her tomorrow, we've got this show to put on tonight and I've got to be at the 81 bus stop by 7 p.m."*

Although John thought the world of Barbara, nothing was going to get in the way of him performing that night. John closed the bedroom door and turned the music down.

He had just spent the previous 20 minutes trying to create some extra curls in his hair at the front, similar to the style of hair of one of his favourite performers; Gene Vincent. He was thinking that this new guy Paul, although quite competent on the guitar would be no threat to rival his own Rock 'n' Roll image. Paul looked a bit old fashioned and respectable, with his neatly combed hair and cherubic face to be a real rocker. John tried on the white jacket which Nigel Whalley had managed to borrow for him to wear. *"Hmmm - not bad,"* he thought as he looked in the mirror, *"though it's not really me but it's different."* This is what seemed to rule John's mind as he would try anything for the sake of being different, anything that caused comment and was a variation on the norm. This was certainly a drastic change in his appearance. He was also thinking of how embarrassed he might feel on the stage in the new outfit knowing full well that he would probably be the target for some nasty jokes and he did not like the idea of being the recipient of humour - he was the one who dished out the jokes.

John went downstairs; Mimi was in the back living room reading a magazine. She looked up as John entered the room.

- *"Have you seen anything of that nice dark haired lad who was at the Garden Fête? You know, the one with the cherubic face."*

- *"Oh Paul, you mean. Yeah, he's in the group now, at least we'll give him a trial run to see what he's like."* Said John nonchalantly, as if he was not really concerned, yet deep down in his heart he was feeling quite apprehensive about teaming up with Paul.

- *"John, I'm not really out to spoil your fun but shouldn't you stay in a bit more than you do and pay a bit more attention to that Barbara. If I were her I would have finished with you long ago, the way you treat her."*

- *"Well you're not her!"retorted* John angrily. *"Now I've got to go."*

With that John quickly ran up to his bedroom, placed his white jacket in a small case, together with a couple of spare guitar strings which he knew he would be needing. He called for Nigel Whalley and they strolled down to the 81 bus stop in Woolton Village.

- *"Nige I'm starving. With all that fuss Mimi was making about me going out tonight I didn't have any tea. Can we get some chips?"*

- *"Yeah okay John, I'll get some with you."* They eventually arrived at the bus stop.

Sometime earlier, 1½ miles away at no.20 Forthlin Road Paul McCartney was sitting in the front room, guitar in hand, practising for what was to be his solo instrumental performance that evening -"Guitar Boogie". He felt assured that he knew the songs pretty well, such as "Twenty Flight Rock" by Eddie Cochrane but was not fully confident about playing the instrumental number.

His father as usual was intent on doing the crossword, which he had been engrossed in for at least half an hour. He looked up disturbed to a degree from his concentration.

- *"What's this for son, are you playing with that new group, what are they called "Quarry Boys?"*

- *"Quarry Men! Dad! Don't be so sarcastic."*

- *"That's a rather strange name, what is it a skiffle group? What are they called that for?"*

- *"It's because they go to the Quarry Bank School. I met the leader of the group last July, a fellow called John Lennon, at the Garden Fête at St Peter's. Don't you remember me telling you about it?"*

- *"Vaguely. I can't seem to keep track of what you are doing these days. I only hope your school work isn't suffering because of it."*

Paul's younger brother, Michael suddenly burst into the room.

- *"Paul take me with you tonight. Ah go on, don't be mean. I could look after your things for you in case they get pinched."*

- *"Don't be stupid Mike, you're far too young. Anyway Dad needs some company."*

Paul was still intent on getting his guitar chords correct.

- *"Paul, will you stop it and relax. If you don't know them by now all this messing about won't help your performance. Anyway I've heard you play that one before and it sounded alright to me."*

- *"Dad it's my first time on stage with this group and I want to get it right."*

- *"Paul, I know how you feel but you have got to have faith in your own ability. There is no substitute for performing on stage live. Look upon it as a form of practice. It's not going to be the end of the world if you get it wrong."*

- *"It is to me."* Paul looked up to the clock on the mantlepiece. *"Crikey Dad, I'll have to go."*

With that he went up to his bedroom clutching his guitar. He looked out of his bedroom window. *"Thank goodness it's not raining,"* he thought as he gathered his white coat from the wardrobe and folded it neatly into a canvass holdall bag, being very conscious of not wanting to get the smart jacket all crumpled by the time the show started. He threw in the song books making sure the book that had the chords to "Guitar Boogie" was there, together with a warm sweater and a few spare guitar strings. He would wear part of the outfit now he thought, as he put on a clean white shirt and a pair of black trousers. It would save some time once he got there, perhaps there might even be enough time to revise the guitar sequence.

He shouted a big "cheerio" to his father and set off to walk to Woolton Village, having decided he would cut across Allerton Golf Links, as it was dry, and it would make the walk shorter by at least half a mile. He eventually arrived at the 81 bus stop at approximately 7 p.m. Already gathered there were John Lennon, Eric Griffiths and Nigel Whalley.

- *"Where's Len?"* he asked.

I had managed to arrive at Nigel Whalley's house by about 6:45 p.m., my intention being to leave my bicycle there and transport the tea chest to the 81 bus stop. I arrived to find that Nigel had already gone with John Lennon and that the tea chest, according to Nigel's father, was not there. Perhaps it was at Ivan Vaughan's, next door, I thought and I knocked on Ivan's door. Ivan appeared.

- *"Hi Len. I thought you were playing tonight. What are you doing here?"*

- *"Look Ivy I'm in a rush. Have you got the tea chest? It's not at Nigel's place."*

- *"Yeah, I've got it, I thought I would touch the paint work up a bit, it was starting to look a bit grotty."*

- *"Ivy can you give me a hand to help me carry it to the 81 bus stop. I'm supposed to meet the others there by 7 p.m."*

- *"Okay, I'll be with you in a tick. Do you want to park your bike around the side?"*

I parked up my bicycle, we collected the tea chest and walked as quickly as we could to the 81 bus stop in the centre of Woolton Village, (which was about half a mile away from Ivan's house). We got there at about ten minutes past 7.

- *"Where the heck have you been Len?"* They all said almost simultaneously. *"We've just missed a bus."*

After explaining the situation they all calmed down. I gave my thanks to Ivan for his help and eventually a bus arrived and the four of us were finally on our way. The two other members of the group; Eric Griffiths and Colin Hanton had arranged to meet us at the Clubmoor Hall, as they had managed to get a lift from a friend.

The journey on the bus was uneventful apart from the usual disdainful look from the bus conductor at the sight of the tea chest bass but I was used to that by now. We arrived at the hall at about 7:50 p.m. having had to change buses at Utting Avenue which was about three miles north along the Ring Road (Queen's Drive). We were due on stage at 9 p.m. and as we entered the building through the side entrance we could hear the sound of a band already performing. Backstage we all sat around nervously, the smokers of our party furiously dragging away at their cigarettes trying to dull our nerves.

Suddenly John Lennon exclaimed, *"Shit - they're not bad but the vocals are chronic,"* (chronic was a term used a lot by the members of the group and meant "rubbish").

The band that was playing was quite professional and were giving a slick performance of Bill Haley's See You Later Alligator, they were getting a response from the audience, made up mostly of teenagers, who were starting to pack the hall.

- *"We're going to sound pretty primitive compared with this lot,"* said John, *"but I wouldn't perform those type of songs if you paid me a million dollars."*

- *"Ssh! Ssh John, not so loud, you know Charlie McBain doesn't like any noise backstage."* Nigel Whalley remarked.

- *"Listen I don't care who hears me."* said John, raising his voice even louder.

I could see that John was starting to get worked up, he didn't like anyone trying to suppress his natural emotions.

- *"Look John, we're far better than that lot vocally now that we've got Paul."* I said encouragingly, *"and the main thing is..."* I paused here, watching the look on John's face - *"you've got me."* I said jokingly. John promptly burst out laughing and the tension slackened out of his face.

Then suddenly Eric Griffiths and Colin Hanton arrived.

- *"What time are we on?"* asked Eric, as they both dumped their gear in the room.

Now it was time for Paul's instrumental performance - "Guitar Boogie". Paul started off quite well but about half way through he seemed to lose confidence and began making a few mistakes. The audience however did not seem to mind, as John Lennon, realising that Paul was having difficulty suddenly brought the number to a halt.

- *"He's our new boy - he'll be alright given time."* John quipped over the microphone.

The audience rocked with laughter. It seemed as though they were half expecting humour to be injected into almost every song; since John had started the performance off in a humorous vein and so what could have been rather an embarrassing moment for Paul and for the whole band was dissipated by Lennon's humour. We finished off our repertoire and received quite rousing applause. Probably not for our rendition of the songs but more likely for the sheer cheekiness of that chap Lennon.

So ended the debut of Paul McCartney teaming up alongside John Lennon.

It seemed to be like the joining of a missing piece in a jigsaw; the last piece to complete the picture had been found and no one realised at the time what a foundation had been laid in terms of popular music history, that was not realised until many years later.

— Len Garry (left) with John Lennon (upside down) - Pete Shotton (right) & Billy Turner's legs —

2

My Early Life:

I was born in Liverpool on the 6th of January 1942, the twelfth day of Christmas. My father, Henry Garry, a printer by trade had married Phyllis Cartwright and had had two sons; the elder named Walter, in 1939, and myself, Leonard Charles. Phyllis, my mother, was the youngest daughter of Walter and Phyllis Cartwright who owned and ran a baby linen store in Woolton Road.

Woolton Road was the road that ran from the Wavertree area of Liverpool, bisected Lance Lane where I lived and ran past Mosspits Lane School. It continued along for three or four miles. Eventually one would arrive at Woolton Village (the significance of this at the time was not apparent to me, but now it seems that even geographically I would be linked with the likes of John Lennon, Pete Shotton and the gang).

I was brought up at No.77 Lance Lane which was a modest, three bedroomed, semi-detached house in the suburb of Wavertree. The house was about five min-

— No: 77 Lance Lane: Len Garry's home —

utes walk away from the baby linen shop in Woolton Road where my grand-parents (on my mother's side) lived and where, during the early thirties, as a young woman, she would help out.

My father, Henry Garry, was a printer by trade and worked as a compositor on the Liverpool Daily Post, having served his time in the merchant navy during the war. I would love listening to the tales of when he was out in New York during the period when the notorious gangster, Al Capone was alive and the prohibition days were active.

My childhood was a happy one. My earliest memory was that of sharing a pram with my brother and being given a banana and trying to eat it with the skin still on. My mother would often have to push us both up the hill from the Penny Lane area with a load of shopping all on one pram. My brother (who was three years older than me) and I, were always fighting, as we were quite different in personality.

I started my education at Mosspits Lane County Primary School, which was about a brisk five minute walk from where I lived. At that time the construction of the new infant's department was just being completed. My earliest memory at infant school was trying to push a rather large girl off a rocking horse as she always seemed to monopolize it. There were times at school that stuck in my

— Mosspits Lane Junior School - Len, Lennon and Shotton's first school —

— The baby linen shop, now 'Ooh La La', where Lens' Grandparents lived. —

memory. I can recall at Christmas time some girls putting on a dancing display and one of the girls was called Wendy McKay. She was a very pretty girl with golden curls and she would dance the Scottish sword dance. I think this must have been my first crush - I was probably about eight years of age.

I can recall sitting in assembly every morning listening to the pianist; Miss 'Fatty' Forester (I will tell of her later on). We would have to sing some stupid songs such as; "Come on you lassies and lads, get leave of your Dads and away to the Maypole high," etc etc. The songs were awful and I judged them to be very sissy-like - this was probably my first real experience of what music was and I was not very interested in it.

I can also remember sitting next to a girl named Carol Lupton who would constantly pinch my legs under the bench seats where we sat as pupils (they were double benches) and as I wore short pants at the time it was becoming unbearable, although I didn't have the heart to tell the teacher. I think my Mum probably sorted it out eventually.

Living nearby I never stayed for school dinners. Thankfully, as the smell of stewed cabbage used to make me feel sick (I used to have a delicate stomach). Every lunchtime at 12 p.m. I would dash home usually to a meal of soup, mashed potato, sausages and beans. I used to listen to a radio show while having lunch called "Workers Playtime" which was a sort of working class variety show. As time went on at school I progressed rather well academically, with no major problems. I was always good at spelling, probably because even at an early age my father would encourage me to read good literature and also, being a printer, he passed his spelling knowledge on to me.

I progressed from the junior school to the seniors when I reached the age of 9 years. My brother Walter also went to the same school but because he was older than me our paths rarely crossed. Unlike myself he was never keen on ball games although he excelled in athletics. I was placed in Miss Whittles' class who was I recall quite an attractive lady in her late twenties (her nickname then was "Miss Whittley Tits").

I was a rather mischievous lad, always full of fun and keen to make a game out of everything. I also enjoyed trying to entertain the class with wisecracks or stunts. I remember one instance of this - I must have been about 10 years old and I was in Miss Whittles' class. It was a hot and sunny afternoon and all the classroom windows had been opened. I happened to look out of the window and spotted a rather large girl, whose name I cannot now remember, make her way rather ponderously along Woolton Road. She happened to be about ten minutes late, I suddenly shouted out loud; *"Hurry up Fatty, you're late again!"*

I was good at most sports, especially cricket. I was not only in the 2nd eleven team but also in the 1st eleven, even though I was strictly speaking too young to be officially included. The headmaster at the time was Mr Webb and I can remember batting at a cricket match, (probably against Dovedale Road School) and hitting the ball straight through the headmaster's window.

Whilst at school, when I reached the age of ten years, I was being targeted by a gang of lads led by a rather rough character called David Holmes. They would gang up on me now and then and try to force me to give them my marbles. Marbles was a game that was constantly being played at the school and involved one lad throwing small coloured glass balls - "ollies" as they were affectionately called, and the other lad throwing his. The object of the game was simply to hit the other lad's "ollie" with your own, in which case it then became yours.

Anyway, the situation was becoming intolerable and this lad, David Holmes, was asking for a showdown. One evening he followed me home to 77 Lance Lane. I told my father that this lad would not leave me alone. *"What do I do Dad?"* I asked. Dad's response was, *"go and sort him out son, there's a grass verge outside"*. So David Holmes and I stood toe to toe out on the grass verge in Lance Lane, I can't recall the exact outcome, but he never bothered me again. The episode apparently got back to the school because I swiftly gained a reputation for being quite a tough guy (I was quite tall for my age at the time).

Due to the overcrowding at Mosspits Lane, some of the classes were transferred to the "Bluecoat School" in Church Road, which was about a ten minute walk away from Lance Lane. It was here that I was confronted by another "bully type". His name was "Fatty Folland". Isn't it strange that everyone with a surname beginning with "F" is given the nickname "Fatty"? Well this lad really was fat! He was also begging for a fight. I suppose that my reputation must have gone before me so he felt that he had something to prove. Now, this lad happened to wear glasses and he was obviously short sighted. When we squared up to one another he fortunately slipped and in doing so broke his glasses. This took the steam out of the situation and everyone looking on thought I had knocked him over. Victory was won without having to lift a finger!

One of my favourite teachers at Mosspits Lane was a certain Mr Roddy. "Pop" Roddy as he was affectionately known was well liked by almost everyone. I think this was because of four main reasons. Firstly, to an impressionable ten year old, images are very important and he was always dressed very smartly, usually wearing a trench-style macintosh - a reminder of the American style detective in the type of movies prevalent at that time. Secondly, he loved cricket and thought that I was a good player (which I was!). Thirdly, I remember that on one occasion he was giving us a spelling test and had asked if anyone in the class could spell a certain, rather difficult, word. I put up my hand and got it right (I was the only one to respond). I got a fair amount of praise and encouragement from this simple little episode. I think it's very important, especially for parents and teachers, to give the right praise and encouragement to those they have responsibility for, it can work wonders! Fourthly, Mr Roddy had a good sense of humour. I can remember one day, when he was walking along one of the side streets directly opposite Bluecoat School on his way back to Mosspits Lane. It was snowing heavily and I threw some snowballs, trying to knock his 'Dick Tracy' type trilby hat off. 'Pop' Roddy returned the fire and joined in the fun. He was a great teacher and I got on with him very well.

Impressions at that age are very important. I was nearing the age when television was about to invade homes across Britain. People were starting to buy more and more electrical goods; rationing was coming to an end and people had more money to spend. New influences were beginning to seep into British society as a result of these increases in media and communications; by telephone, radio, television etc. I can remember seeing my first television programme at my grandfather Garry's house in West Derby. It was a black and white programme called "Sooty and Sweep" - the invasion had started! This would develop into a group of influences which was to help form the attitudes of a group of lads who were to change the musical (and some would say political) world.

Mr Roddy was our cricket coach at Mosspits. Now, our cricket pitch must have been one of the worst in the world. It's still there today. One afternoon we happened to be entertaining Rudston Road School in a match. "Pop" Roddy put me on to bowl. The pitch was very, very bumpy, it looked more like the surface of the moon than the smooth grassy pitch it should have been. Anyway, I took about three wickets in nine balls and was applauded with shouts of, "well done Garry!" Needless to say that we won the match handsomely and everyone thought that I had bowled very well. I failed to understand how it had never dawned on the players, coach and company that the pitch had been unplayable. It seemed to me that I was succeeding in gaining victories in life, whether in fights or sport, that required very little effort on my part.

The Influence of Music

I developed a love of music quite early on in my life, probably through listening to my grandfather's records at the Baby Linen Shop at 113 Woolton Road.

— Len Garry's grandparents. —

I would listen to the Ink Spots, Bing Crosby and Frank Sinatra on grandfather Cartwright's wind up gramophone. I must admit that I preferred Sinatra, as his voice seemed to have a lot more life in it. I also liked The Ink Spots for their harmonies and soft tones.

There used to be a grand reunion of the "Cartwight" side of the family at Christmas time (reminiscent of "Bonanza" only without the horses). My mother had two sisters, one called Vivian who was older and one called Elizabeth who was younger. Vivian was married to a Royal Navy officer, "Uncle Fred" and Elizabeth or "Betty" was courting a young Scottish student and finishing a

— Len Garry with parents. —

degree at University. There was also cousin John, who was the son of Auntie Viv. They would all be there at Christmas time. I loved these get-togethers. Grandfather Cartwright would be seated at the head of the table and would dominate the proceedings. He would always carve the turkey and I couldn't help but notice that he would always seem to get the best bits. He would always "say grace" before the meal and afterwards we would all play Monopoly, sitting around the large mahogany table. I would sit next to my mother and as I was only 9 or 10 at the time I knew that if I was losing and looked like being counted out of the game, I could always rely on Mum to slip me £500 under the table, thereby preventing me from bursting into tears. I hated losing anything that was competitive.

— Len Garry with his brother Walter —

Sometimes my brother Walter and myself would sleep over at Woolton Road, as there were sleeping quarters up above the shop. One of the pranks that we would get up to was to tie black twine to the door knockers of adjoining shops and then tie the other end to the support posts of the canopy which ran across the full length of the shopping parade, hoping that a passer by would break the twine and thereby inadvertently operate the knocker. It never seemed to work, much to our dismay! It was probably just as well, as my grandfather Cartwright always appeared a rather austere person to me, he didn't seem to laugh much.

We loved to play with the gramophone, often turning up the speed of the records, as we were fascinated by the change of pitch; Bing Crosby singing "White Christmas" as though he were high on "speed". My brother Walter and I would often imitate these singers as we lay in our beds at No. 77 (we shared the back bedroom in our early years).

My mother was musical. She was an accomplished pianist, could read music well and had a good singing voice. Quite often there would be a sing - song on a Sunday evening, when my Uncle Jack would sing duets with my mother around the piano. Jack and Mum would sing mainly Ivor Novello songs such as "We'll Gather Lilacs in the Spring Again".

— Len Garry's parents —

My mother, in order to help out with the family budget, would work as a hairdresser in our home, doing friends' and neighbours' hair as she was a qualified hairdresser. This would involve the ladies sitting under the large hair dryer that was on our first floor landing; it looked like something from outer space, as did the dear ladies as they emerged from the dryer with the large rollers in their hair. I would often help out my mother by passing her paper tissues for her to perm their hair. The ammonia smell was pretty awful, however I braved the smell as I would often get a tip from the old ladies.

My music teacher at primary school was a rather large, single lady called Miss Forester. Now, as it happened, our back garden at Lance Lane overlooked the back garden of this lady, although there was about 100 yards distance between the two. One of my pranks would be to shoot dried peas, (I was very thoughtful, I never used stones), by catapult directly into her back garden - trying also to ping her rear end as she shoveled up her coal.

Not content with this I would tie thin black twine to my next door neighbour's door knocker (who also happened to be a retired teacher) and thread it through my bedroom window, then I would lie in bed pulling the twine. Fortunately for me it did not seem to bother the poor lady, who I later realised was as deaf as a doorpost.

Back at school I was unaware at the time that two boys who were to play an important part in my early teenage life also had links with the school. According to the records, John Lennon had been enrolled as a pupil, probably shortly after he had been born and was then living in Newcastle Road, which was not far from Lance Lane. Mosspits Lane would have been the nearest primary school at the time. Also, a lad called Pete Shotton attended Mosspits Lane as a pupil. I was younger than Peter and so I don't remember him at school.

I was encouraged to learn piano at an early age under my mother's influence. We had inherited an upright piano - a "Steck" from Grandfather Cartwright, as he had recently passed away. I struggled on the piano, although I found the theory of music very boring and the exercises I was given to do even more boring. My teacher, who happened to be one of my mother's hairdressing clients, was very, very large (even larger than Fatty Forester). She had a very domineering manner and would stand immediately behind me as I sat at the piano for my weekly music lesson. She would say, "keep those wrists up Leonard and watch the metronome". It was all becoming too much for me. However I did very slowly manage to reach the standard of playing the "Blue Danube". Eventually I gave up the classes but I can still remember her little ways of trying to teach me musical theory such as E,G,B,D,F, (Every Good Boy Deserves Fruit). This lady also taught elocution lessons and my brother Walter was one of her pupils. He went on to win the Liverpool Cup for reciting the poem by Walter de la Mare, "The Plumber."

In fact it was so successful that Walter was asked to perform the poem at Mosspits Lane end of term show. I was very proud of my brother at the time. It also struck me as very strange that this enormous lady had glass houses in her music room that housed her stick insects. They were so thin and camouflaged that you could hardly see them - what a contrast!

Life at Lance Lane was pretty hard in the winter time. The whole of Britain were still using ration books and we were only allowed a limited number of coupons for sweets, sugar, bacon, butter etc. Sometimes when the weather was very cold my mother would heat up two stone irons on the stove (irons normally used for ironing clothes), wrap them up in an old blanket and put them in our beds in order to warm our beds up. Unfortunately, on some occasions they would be so hot that the blankets would burn and I would wake up to see the bedclothes smouldering, still at least we were warm!

Popular music was being listened to more and more and I was given a combined radio / record player for Christmas one year. I would listen to radio Luxembourg's Top Twenty late on Saturday nights with artists such as Pat Boone, Guy Mitchell and Frankie Laine, who all made an impression on me. I was more aware now that I really did have the gift of a good singing voice and my interest in popular music grew.

At the age of eleven in June 1953, I passed the eleven plus examination which determined whether I would go to a Grammar School or a Secondary Modern. The Grammar was considered better academically and on passing the exam I was given my first choice of school which was the Liverpool Institute High School. Quarrybank High School was second on my list although I would have liked it to have been my first choice because it was situated in a nice part of Liverpool and it had a good sporting reputation. The Institute had a better reputation for academic achievement.

The Liverpool Institute was on Mount Street near the heart of the City of Liverpool which was about 4 miles from where I lived in the suburbs. This meant me having to get the No. 73 bus which stopped on Heathfield Road on the corner of Lance Lane. In wintertime I remember feeling very cold on the buses. In those days, there was no entrance door and the buses were open to the cold outside air and had no heating. They would be crammed full in the mornings with loads of school kids, boys and girls journeying to the City, as quite a number of the good grammar schools were situated within the inner city area.

The Liverpool Institute was quite a frightening building to an eleven year old who was used to the more homely surroundings of a suburban primary school. The entrance doors were huge and the whole scale of the building gave you a sense of awe as you stepped through the portals. The rooms were huge, with massive windows, the decor was very dark with lots of brown hardwood and it seemed to be dark everywhere, creating a miserable and oppressive atmosphere.

All the new boys including myself had been "kitted out" in our brand new uniform which was a black and green cap, grey socks with black and green bands and grey short trousers. On our black blazer was our badge which had the school motto depicted in Latin, "Non nobis solum sed totum mundo nati". Translated as, "Not for ourselves alone but for the whole world."

There were no playing fields at the Institute as the school was situated in the inner city area. There was a playground of concrete slabs surrounded on all sides by a very high cast iron railing. Directly linked next door was the College of Art building. The whole place reminded me more of a penitentiary than a place of learning.

The headmaster's name was J.R. Edwards or "Bas" as we called him, (I have since realised that his nickname was short for "bastard"). It was quite an apt name for him at the time however, today maybe it might have been toned down to merely "J.R.", who knows? He had a miserable face, hardly ever smiled and would twitch his mouth and shift from one leg to the other when he was angry, which seemed to be his permanent state. Every morning the whole school would meet for morning assembly to say prayers and sing a few hymns. The headmaster would arrive on the platform dressed up in a black gown with his black mortar board perched precariously on his bald head. I did not find it a very pleasant atmosphere.

I was placed in form 3A at the Liverpool Institute and my form master was Mr J.E.Watson. He was also my Latin teacher. He was another person who seemed to blend in well with the general atmosphere; he hardly ever smiled, walked with a very straight back and seemed to be made of other stuff than flesh and blood - more like cast iron. No wonder I sought out friends who would lighten up the atmosphere for me, people with whom I could have a laugh, I met one in particular; Ivan Vaughan. We soon became friends and although he was keen to get on well, he had a similar sense of humour and was game for a laugh most of the time. It was this zany humour that was the main link of friendship between us.

Often, Ivan and I would say to the games master before gymnastics sessions (which we both hated), "Spasms Sir, Spasms". I never really knew what this meant but it frightened the games master sufficiently to let us watch gloatingly from the balcony, as the rest of the class were being made to cavort and exercise to the limits of their ability. Little did I know at the time that Ivan must have got the term "spasms" from his friend, Nigel Whalley, who I had not yet met. Nigel Whalley was subject to very bad asthma attacks.

I did well at the Institute in the first years, usually coming within the top three in the class and progressing up to 4B. Ivan did particularly well in the classics, such as Latin and Greek. In 1955 we were split into different classes; Ivan taking classics and I taking modern languages.

Meanwhile life at home was fairly uneventful, apart from the fact that my father went onto night shift in order to earn more money, my mother was still working part time as a hairdresser. My brother Walter had been thrown out of the Bluecoat School for shaving his head bald. He seemed to hang around with rather strange friends and had even stranger tastes in music.

Walter would often bring one of his friends back home to play on the piano in our front room. This friend was rather unfortunate in being heavily pimpled with mousey greasy hair, wore thick-lensed glasses and smoked like a chimney. Occasionally, I would poke my head into the room and would almost be knocked over by the smoky, foggy air. This fellow would be banging out some Beethoven symphony while my brother Walter would be lying on the floor listening in a deep, trance like state. My taste in music went in entirely the opposite direction, as did the type of friends that I became involved with.

I loved going to the pictures. I would often go twice a week, depending on my financial situation, I had only just turned thirteen around this time. The cinema or the "pictures" as we used to call it, was a necessary form of escapism for me as I had not yet linked up with the likes of John Lennon, Pete Shotton and company. I would go to the Abbey Cinema, often on a Monday night as the Abbey was only ten minutes away from where I lived. My favourite films were those such as; "Moonlight Bay", or "Carousel" or comedies with music such as the Dean Martin and Jerry Lewis films. I would try to remember the words of the songs and sing to myself as I walked back home. It never occurred to me that I might be lonely. I quite enjoyed going about on my own, Ivan Vaughan lived quite a distance away and so I never bothered to travel to meet him at that point in time.

Finally I asked my parents for a record player for Christmas. By this time I had moved into the small bedroom at the front of the house and unfortunately there was no electric socket in the bedroom for me to plug my new record player into. I therefore used to plug it into the landing, which was also used to plug in my mother's hairdresser's dryer. Sometimes I would be in my bedroom listening to Radio Luxembourg or Radio Caroline (which were the best popular music stations) and my mother would need to use the drying machine for her clients. I would give way of course but afterwards, those "dear ladies" would have to put up with me playing the new music songs, mostly from America such as Guy Mitchell, Pat Boone etc.

On Sundays we always had a roast dinner usually with apple pie or home made custard tarts for dessert. Sometimes I would make my Mum and Dad a cup of tea and toast as they were lazing on Sunday mornings. I can remember carrying the tea and toast up the stairs, often spilling the tea into the saucer as I carried it. I would pause at the bedroom door and transferred the tea hastily back into the cups before entering the bedroom. Sunday lunch was enjoyable and I was particularly fond of rhubarb tart, as the rhubarb was grown fresh in our back garden.

Lance Lane was a through route for the mounted police horses when they made their journey from Mather Avenue Police Training Centre to the Liverpool and Everton Football Club matches. On their way down Lance Lane they would relieve themselves and Dad would say, *"Len, get out there with the shovel quick and we'll put it on the rhubarb"*. After that Dad's favourite joke would be, *"what do we put on our rhubarb son?"* I would answer, *"Custard, Dad!"* He would then say, *"Nay lad, we put horse manure on ours."*

On Sunday afternoons I would usually go to Sunday school class at St Stephen's Presbyterian Church on the corner of Lance Lane from 2:30 p.m. to 3:30 p.m., while Mum and dad had their afternoon snooze. Afterwards, I would usually go with a friend to Calderstones Park to play football. On Sunday afternoons in the summertime one would see a steady procession of couples - some married, pushing their new prams along Lance Lane and across Dudlow Lane which led directly to the northern entrance of Calderstones Park. It was a very pleasant walk, tree lined all the way, passing some lovely houses with large front gardens, all showing off their summer blooms. I grew to love Calderstones Park very much.

Early Days at the Liverpool Institute

At the Institute when I was about 14 years old, Ivan Vaughan and I were split into different classes. It was while I was in the German set that I first became acquainted with Paul McCartney, who had also become friends with Ivan Vaughan. Paul, from my memory, was a very able student and seemed to grasp the rudiments of the German language very quickly. I meanwhile, struggled.

Most of the teachers at the Institute were given nicknames by us. I can remember a few of them even now. There was "Weepy Walker", the science teacher, who had an unfortunate habit of spraying students with his saliva when pronouncing the letter "p". As a result it was no surprise that students would make a dash for the back row seats as soon as they entered his lesson, in order to avoid being "sprayed". All the front seats would remain vacant.

There was also "Johnnie Wray". We called him this after the American singer Johnnie Rae who had just brought out a hit record called "Cry". This was to be a very apt nickname, I will explain why. One day Mr Wray, who was fairly new to the school, was setting up a scientific experiment. It was obviously his first experience of teaching the "creme de la creme" of students. In setting up the experiment he accidentally cut himself, drawing blood from a rather nasty cut. We burst out laughing and poor Mr Wray couldn't take any more and burst into tears. The nickname therefore became even more appropriate. We were a cruel bunch in those days.

Ivan Vaughan lived in Vale Road in a semi detached house called "Vega" just off Menlove Avenue. After I got to know Ivan quite well at the age of thirteen, he invited me over to meet a new friend. I went over one day in early August 1955, the name of the boy I was to meet was John Winston Lennon.

3

Meeting John Lennon and the Gang:

World Events in 1955

The year 1955 was, as far as the world scene goes quite eventful. Sir Winston Churchill had to resign through ill health and passed on the mantle to Anthony Eden who was a much younger man. He in turn inherited a commonwealth that was beginning to rebel against British rule, such as the Mau Mau movement in Kenya.

Racial issues were always in the forefront of the news, with black Americans demonstrating peacefully in an attempt to assert their rights.

In the cinematic sphere the "Blackboard Jungle" starring Glenn Ford helped to put Rock 'n' Roll on the world stage with it's theme song "Rock around the Clock" by Bill Haley and the Comets. In the sports arena the U.K.'s Donald Campbell smashed the world water speed record on July 23rd. It seemed as though it was the year for breaking records as the American Country and Western singer Slim Whitman lasted eleven weeks at number one in the British pop charts with "Rose Marie".

It was also the year the teenage heart throb James Dean died in a tragic car accident at the age of twenty four, after having made such classic films as "East of Eden" and 'Rebel Without a Cause". Dean's crash happened on September 30th, only weeks after I met John Lennon.

Meeting with John Lennon and "The Gang"

Liverpool, August 1955

It was a bright sunny day in early August and Liverpool was experiencing one of it's warmest summers for many years. It was during the school holidays and I had been away from the Liverpool Institute for a week. Before the school had broken up my friend Ivan Vaughan had given me an invitation to come over and meet his friend, John Lennon. It is strange because I can still remember his exact words. Perhaps small things that are about to make a large impact on your life are more easily remembered, phrases that were spoken, smells, a piece of music that had a great impact on you, a person that leaves a strong impression in your mind, all these things can leave a lasting imprint on your mind and recalling them brings you back to your past.

I decided to take up Ivan's invitation early that Saturday afternoon. Prior to this time my circle of friends had naturally been confined to the area where I was living which was the Wavertree area of Liverpool, friends that I had grown up with prior to my teens; those that I had met at Mosspits Lane first school, such as Billy Turner.

- *"Where are you off to now son?"* asked my Dad, who, although still working nights had appeared in the garden wearing his slippers. I was pumping up the tires on my Raleigh Rudge bicycle which I had had for two years now, ever since I had passed my 11 plus in order to be accepted into the Liverpool Institute.

- *"I thought you were going to help me with the ladders so I could clean the gutters?"*

- *"Oh yeah, sorry Dad but can't it wait till Sunday? You're off then aren't you? It's just that Ivan Vaughan, my friend from school has invited me over. I was going to go last week only I helped you out with the painting remember?"*

- *"No I don't remember but go on then, you're only young once. I think it's a good idea for you to widen your circle of friends. Just make sure they're decent, your Mum and I get very concerned that you don't associate with the wrong sort of company."*

- *"I know Dad - don't worry. My friend Ivan studies all the time and he lives in a nice area of Liverpool. Hey guess what? He got a Raleigh Rudge for passing the 11 plus like me."*

- *"I bet he takes more care of it than you do. When was the last time you cleaned or oiled it?"*

- *"Give us a chance Dad. We've only been broken up a week, I'll have a go at it tomorrow."*

- *"Everything with you is tomorrow. Tomorrow never comes, remember that."* Dad was renowned for his wise platitudes.

- *"What's the time? Oh no, it's nearly 2 o'clock and I've got to cycle all the way to Menlove Avenue."*

- *"All the way! Bah! It's not that far, why, it's only just past Calderstone's Park.*

Your mother and I walked that distance quite regularly."

- *"If I don't go now I'll miss meeting them."* I said. *"Cheerio."*

With that I wheeled my bike through the recently built, car-less garage, into Lance Lane. I wondered why my Dad had had that garage built when all it housed was his tools and the ladder. I thought garages were built to put cars into. I cycled down Lance Lane, crossed over Heathfield Road (which leads down to Penny Lane) and entered the beautifully tree lined Dudlow Road. It was quite rare for me to ride my bicycle as far as Calderstones as the friends I "knocked about" with at that time rarely seemed to want to use their bicycles. I think I was feeling a little nervous as I turned into Menlove Avenue. I was wondering why Ivan was so anxious for me to meet his friends, as it seemed like a rather unusual request. Friends came about in the natural process of life. Perhaps he wants to show me off to them? No, my big headed thought was dismissed instantly.

I was about 15 minutes into my journey and already half way up Menlove Avenue, the bike was running perfectly, I wondered what Ivan's Raleigh Rudge would be like, would it be the same colour and style as mine? This seemed a very important matter to me at the time. I was the sort of person who always tried to find links, things that were commonly shared and yet had not been pre-planned. If I did find any "links" it was like a sign to me that whatever it was was meant to be.

I passed the main entrance of Calderstones Park, which was on the right hand side of the road where the circle of Calderstones looked as if they were standing guard over the entrance. I was now on the home straight, I'd be there in about ten minutes. I passed by some beautiful detached houses on my left which faced on to the park. Hey - wait a minute I passed a recognisable house. It belonged to an acquaintance more than a friend who I used to play cricket with in Mosspits Lane School. A guy called Anthony Zalin. I must have been about ten at the time and I came to his house once to play a game of cricket across the way. Another link? No, no, just a co-incidence.

I passed by the house at about twelve miles per hour and looked briefly to see if I could recognize anyone but saw no one I knew, so I kept on peddling. On my immediate right, as I approached Beaconsfield Road where the tennis courts were I could see people in white dashing about the courts. It had never appealed to me; tennis, it didn't seem like a man's game. Men's games were cricket, football and rugby.

Suddenly I was approaching Vale Road, Ivan had told me that it was the next one after Beaconsfield Road but hadn't mentioned that it was actually about 200 yards away.

I had never ventured up this area, by bicycle or by bus, so it was completely virgin territory to me and the only person I knew here was Ivan Vaughan. I wonder if he'll be in? He had told me to look for a sign saying 'Vega" on the front of the houses. I turned down Vale Road. Phew, I thought as I peddled on.

At a distance of around 20 yards I could see a group of teenagers walking down Vale Road, just passing a place where a tree predominates a bend in the road. It was Ivan, and with him three other lads, all with their bicycles.

— The corner of Vale Road 'by the tree' where Len met Lennon for the first time. —

- *"Hi there Len!"* Shouted Ivan, who was the only one who knew me.

- *"You made it up here at last. I thought you were going to come last Saturday. Anyway, it's good to see you."*

Ivan introduced me to his friends who had stopped and were standing around the pavement; Nigel Whalley, Pete Shotton and John Lennon.

- *"Hang on a minute, I know you don't I?"* Asked Pete Shotton, *"didn't you go to Mosspits Lane School. Yeah, I've seen you in the cricket team."*

I thought back for a moment then remembered a gangling youth with white curly hair who used to wait to meet his mother at "going home time" (Pete was usually picked up by car).

- *"Oh yeah, I have seen you at Mosspits. Hi Pete."*

Ivan then introduced me to a lad that had been hovering in the background. I looked at him, his expression; it was that of a rather shy, tousled haired youth, smaller than me and a little stockier in build. He had a quizzical expression, as though he was assessing my credentials as a person, I could almost feel his gaze penetrating me.

- *"Hi I'm John."* He said in a rather sarcastic tone.

This was my first introduction to John Lennon. I made some remark about it being a co-incidence that his bike was a Raleigh Lenton - a name similar to the surname "Lennon".

- *"Yeah, it's strange isn't it? As though it was made for me!"* He replied and suddenly his face was transformed as he gave an infectious giggle.

I noticed that he had something in his hand that looked like a notebook or a school exercise book.

- *"Show Len your cartoons,"* said Ivan, who seemed to be quite anxious that we 'hit it off' with one another and the conversation wasn't flowing that well at the time.

John showed me the book in which he had drawn characterisations of some of his Quarry Bank teachers. I looked through it briefly. In it were also drawings of a strange looking being with two or three heads and as I read further there was the title, "The story of Davy Crutch Head". This was a satirical view of the American hero Davy Crocket, about whom there had recently been a hit record. I was quite impressed. We then chatted for a while about our musical tastes.

It never occurred to me that this "gang" of teenagers were a very close knit group and for me to get on with them so well was a miracle. I felt as though my sense of humour, the disdain with which I beheld education and teachers and my similar taste in music, were all things that we held in common.

- *"Where were you off to?"* I asked, because I felt that I was intruding into their plans for the afternoon.

- *"Well, we waited for you for a while ,"* said Ivan *"and because we thought you weren't coming we were all going to go to the swimming baths in Woolton Village."*

- *"You go on and do that,"* I said, *"and I'll see you next week."*

- *"No"* said John, *"we can't all go to the baths seeing as you came all this way to see Ivan. I know, we three will go; Pete, Nigel and myself. You and Ivan could go over to his place. I know that he has said a lot about you to us — and to his Mum."*

I immediately sensed that this guy John was the leader of the group and I appreciated the fact that even though I could see that he was someone who liked to poke fun in people, there also appeared to be a caring side to his nature. Finally Ivan and I decided to go back to his place in Vale Road while the others collected their swimming gear and went on their way.

— 'Vega' Vale Road - Ivan Vaughan's house near to 'Mendips'. —

Ivan and I talked as we sauntered back to "Vega".

- *"So these are your famous friends. They're okay. That fellow, what's his name,*

John Lennon. He seems like a decent enough sort."

- *"Oh John, yeah, he's great fun to be with, you'll get to know him better in time."*

We were now back at Ivan's house. Ivan introduced me to his mother and I was invited in for a cup of tea. It was such a pleasant afternoon that Ivan and I took our tea out to the back garden.

- *"Did you know that my garden backs on to John Lennon's back garden?"*
- *"Now how could I possibly know that? I've never even been to John's house. Where does he live?"*

- *"He lives in Menlove Avenue in a place called Mendips with his Aunt Mimi."*

- *"Hasn't he got a mother then?"*

- *"Yeah but his mother left his real father. Or was it the other way around? Anyway, his Aunt thought it would be better if John lived with her."*

- *"Gosh, I think I would be devastated if that happened in my life. Does he ever go to see his real Mum?"*

- *"Yeah, but he's only found out recently where his real Mum lives, in Springwood not far from where he's living now. John's Aunt Mimi's brother is no other than Cissie Smith, our English teacher!"*

- *"No! I don't believe it. Well, well. I had better be on my best behaviour in English in future, you never know what gets spread around."*

Just then Ivan's mother came into the garden.

- *"Where have all the other boys gone to?"* she asked. *"I thought they were with you?"*

Ivan explained that I didn't have any swimming trunks and that they had arranged to go swimming and so Ivan had stayed with me.

- *"In that case,"* she said *"would you mind doing the garden over a little bit because the weeds are growing fast."*

- *"No, I don't mind."* I said and immediately thought of my Dad struggling with the ladders on his own at home and felt a bit guilty, I could have helped him after all.

Never mind, I'd be able to help him on Sunday. We finished our tea and then set to on the garden from about 3:30 p.m. until about 4:30 p.m. when it was time for me to head back to Lance Lane.

- *"Wait a minute, before you go,"* said Ivan *"I want to show you something."*

He took me to the bottom of his garden , which backed onto Mendips. He showed me a tree on which had been rigged a piece of rope, the rope was con-nected to a tree in John Lennon's back garden.

- *"Look Len, John and I have rigged up this contraption. What we do is we loop a tin can on the string, put a message in it such as "hello" then I climb up the tree and send it through to John. He then sends the can back with a message in. We have to be careful that we don't put any swear words in though, in case Mum or his Aunt Mimi finds out."*

- *"Well, well,"* (that's a waste of time I thought) *"that's great Ivy, but can't you think of anything better to say than "hello" ?"*

- *"Nah, it's just the novelty of the thing."*

I looked at my watch, it was nearing 4:30 p.m. and I was due back for tea at 5 p.m. I said my farewells to Mrs Vaughan and thanked her for the tea, she in turn thanked me for my help in the garden and then I set out for home. Before departing I arranged to meet Ivan the following Monday in order to continue my newly formed friendship with "the gang".

As I headed back along Menlove Avenue towards home I was thinking that I hadn't had much time to get to know John, Pete and company. Well, never mind there were still about six weeks of summer holidays in which I could do that. I arrived home at Lance Lane just as my Mum was putting the tea on the table.

In those days there were very fixed meal times. If I had arrived back at 5:30 I would have missed my tea. Whatever was put in front of you you had to eat or go hungry. These days of course things have changed, there is so much more freedom for teenagers and children, as they usually help themselves to every-thing available. I suppose it was because we did not have the luxury of a refrig-erator and there was no way of preserving food once it had been prepared and one thing that my parents hated was wasting food.

I walked in the house after parking my bicycle just outside the gate. Mum and dad were in the dining room about to start the tea.

- *"Hmm, I can smell kippers."* (Smoked herring).

- *"Len, can you help yourself, just put yourself a pair under the grill."*

I did this, then Mum spotted the oil on my white socks.

- *"Len you've got oil all over your socks from riding your bike. How on earth am I going to get that off?"*

- *"That's because it shows up on white socks Mum. Perhaps I should have worn my black ones instead."* Was my cheeky reply.

In order to keep the bottom of my trousers from catching in the chain of the bicycle I would wear bicycle clips that went around the trousers to keep them tight, but unfortunately exposed the socks which had rubbed on the oily bike chain.

- *"Anyway Dad was saying that I don't oil my bike often enough, didn't you Dad?"*

- *"Don't be cheeky son. Just get a wash and eat your tea. By the way, Mum and I are going out to the Abbey cinema tonight to see a film. Will you be okay?"*

- *"Yeah, don't worry I'll be fine, but I might go for another ride on my bike."*

Mum and Dad went out that night and I was left to decide what to do with my evening. I know, I could pop around to Billy Turner's house, which was only about ten minutes away. Mum and Dad left at about 6 p.m. and I washed up the dishes. Mum had left me two shillings in case I needed a drink or felt like a bag of chips, for which I was grateful.

I wondered whether Billy would be in. Then I remembered that Billy lived just near the Abbey Cinema and Mum and Dad might see me cycling back from his house, they wouldn't be pleased as Billy was still a "taboo" subject for them. I quickly looked in the Liverpool Echo to see whether it was a double feature (two films). It was thankfully, so my parents would be out until about 10:30 and I could make sure that I avoided seeing them.

I cycled around to Billy Turner's at around 7:30 p.m.. Fortunately Billy was in when I arrived. He lived in a semi-detached house in Childwall Road about 100 yards from the Abbey Cinema. We went into his front room. Billy Turner had become a friend of mine when he was introduced to me by another pupil (Peter Roberts) at Mosspits Lane School two years earlier. One of my mother's hair-dressing clients was Mrs Roberts and my Mum would visit her in her own home in order to do her hair.

Billy was small and stocky in stature, with a mass of dark red curly hair and his face was covered in freckles. We nicknamed him "Tubby Turner". Billy had also managed to pass the eleven plus examination and like myself was a pupil at the Liverpool Institute, so the friendship continued.

- *"Bill, I met some great new people this afternoon. I went to Ivan Vaughan's house on Menlove Avenue and he introduced me to some of his mates. "*

- *"It's a bit far to go to get mates isn't it?"*

- *"Yeah I know but I had promised Ivan that I would go and I'm glad that I went now."*

I then mentioned the names of all the new people I had met, including John Lennon and Pete Shotton.

- *"I know Pete Shotton, he used to be a mate of mine at Mosspits."* He said in surprise. *"What school is he going to now?"*

- *"Oh Quarrybank, he doesn't live far from there. Why don't you come along when I go to meet them next week?"*

- *"I might do that. Anyway, what shall we do tonight?"*

- *"Well, we can't go to the pictures, at least not to the Abbey, 'cos my Mum and Dad have gone there, we could just go for a stroll down the High Street and see if we bump into any good looking women."*

- *"Yeah, alright then."*

Ten minutes later Bill and I sauntered down Wavertree High Street looking for nice looking women to bump into. At the age of 13 (Billy was 14), our young hormones were developing and we looked for any contact with the opposite sex we could find or manufacture. We would approach some nice looking woman, suddenly I would push Bill and he would stumble forward towards the unsus-pecting lady. In order to steady himself he would put his hands up, with the intention of placing them on her protruding bits. We spent half an hour down the High Street that night then returned to the house where he made me a cup of tea. I headed for home about 9:30 p.m.

Billy Turner had now been indirectly introduced to "the gang" although he was yet to meet most of them personally.

The next Sunday was a "lie in" day for the Garry family, as it was for many others. Nobody in those days worked on Sundays apart from those that worked in the newsagents that opened for a short while in the mornings. However, as my father was still working the night shift he would sometimes have to work Sunday nights, leaving for work at about 5:00 p.m. While my father had a "lie-in", my brother Walter would be doing his yoga exercises and my mother and I would arise at about 9:30 a.m. to make the breakfasts. This usually consisted of porridge or cornflakes, followed by bacon and eggs with fried bread and tomatoes. Sunday mornings was also the time when my Mum would do the family washing. We had no washing machine or spin drier. Mum would have to boil up the water in a large tub then transfer the large items to be rinsed in the bathroom upstairs. She would then have to pass the soaking wet washing through the mangle in order to dry it (a system of rollers that squeezed the excess water out of the clothes). It was hard work; at the same time the Sunday lunch had to be prepared. Sunday was supposed to be a day of rest but not in the Garry household!

My brother, at the age of sixteen, had enrolled in the Liverpool Art College on Mount Street, after having been accepted on the recommendation of his old art teacher at Bluecoat School and on the strength of his excellent portfolio. He rarely seemed to help about the house. This used to annoy everyone as it meant that everything was left to Mum, although I would help out whenever I could.

Monday arrived: it was another sunny day and I remembered that I had planned to meet Ivan and "the gang" again and I was looking forward to it. We had arranged to meet at Calderstones Park, at the boating shed at the side of the park at 2:00 p.m.

Calderstones Park to me was one of the most beautiful parks on earth. When you entered you seemed to walk in to another world, you were transported far away from all thoughts of Liverpool; it's docks, it's slums, the hustle and bustle of city life. I also felt that it was frequented by a better class of people than the larger Sefton Park. It played an important part in the Quarrymen story too, so I have decided to include a mini history of the park itself.

Calderstones Park - A historical Note:

Calderstones Park was bought from a private land owner (the widow of Charles Maciver, a well known Liverpool ship owner of the Cunard line) by the City of

Liverpool Council in 1902. The price paid for the estate was £43,000 and the corporation gave the property the name Calderstones Park, probably because the large mansion house that was part of the estate was always known as "The Calderstones". In my time this mansion house was always used as a café.

Immediately facing the entrance off Menlove Avenue there was a triangular area of grass that was enclosed by railings. In the centre of this plot of grass was a tall fir tree and this was surrounded by six huge stones, (there were also six in the original line up of the Quarrymen!). These were the Calderstones and they were the oldest relics of antiquity in the area and possibly in the whole of Lancashire. They have for hundreds of years constituted one of the boundary points of the ancient manor of Allerton and were just within the modern limits of another ancient township of Woolton. At this point four roads converge and three ancient manors meet; that of Wavertree to the north, Little Woolton to the east and Allerton to the west.

— A view of the ancient Calderstones in Calderstones Park —

Here to me is another link; John Lennon and Pete Shotton resided in the Woolton area, as did Ivan Vaughan, Nigel Whalley, Eric Griffiths and Rod Davies. I lived in the Wavertree area as did Billy Turner. Paul McCartney lived in the Allerton area. As the roads were to meet; so were we.

To what race or period of history these stones can be assigned we can't account for satisfactorily through man's written history, which only goes back a few hundred years. You would need to go back past the Norman Conquest, past the Saxon occupation in the 6th century A.D. past the invasion of England by Julius Caesar in 55 B.C., past even the Britons and Druids and right back to the Neolithic Age. Here it may be apt to include a few lines from the poet William Roscue who wrote about the stones in 1934.

"Weary with wandering, near this sloping bank
That skirts the brown and solitary heath
I lay me down upon the thymy turf
Beside the mouldering stones, the silent tomb
Of the ancient hunter or the tumulus of warrior bold
Quiet and undisturbed, beneath the waving fern
Their relics lie, and on their sheltered bone
In frequent whirls, thick fell the autumnal leaf."

Someone was digging near these stones in 1764 and found some urns of clay containing the relics of cremated bodies. The evidence of this is made by Edward Baines, a local historian who recorded an account in the Allerton Gazette in 1824, quote;

"In this township, close by the farm on which the famous Allerton oak stands, and just at the point where four ways meet are a quantity of remains called Calderstones, they have the appearance of those stones which are usually regarded as Druidical remains. They bear traces of rude characters which have never been deciphered and from the circumstance of digging about them, urns made from the coarsest clay, containing human dust and bones have been discovered. There is reason to believe that they indicate an ancient burying place."

In 1845 the stones were set up in a vertical position and enclosed by Joseph Need Walker (the builder of the mansion house called Calderstones) within iron railings, and a tree was planted in the centre. They consisted then of six red sandstones, rough on their surfaces, irregular in shape and varying in size from about 3ft by 2ft to about 6ft by 5ft.

In the park, at the time when I frequented it, there stood between the house and the Calderstones themselves an ancient oak tree. It was said to be the place where about 1000 years ago ancient court procedures would take place relating to the old Allerton manor. These stones have now been scattered, some are still in Calderstones Park, protected from vandals in a secure green house near the botanical greenhouses. Another exists in Booker Avenue, not far from where I live now.

— The ancient oak in Calderstones Park —

These stones are a constant reminder to me when I see them of my friendship with the gang long ago.

I arrived at this particular entrance at 1:45p.m., scooted off my bicycle and entered the park. I wonder if they'll be there yet? I thought as I strolled down the narrow pathway that led to the open area of grass that skirted the boating lake. I reached into the pocket of my corduroy jacket, (this was a jacket that I had borrowed from my brother Walter), for my five Senior Service pack which I had bought with the two shillings my mother had given me a couple of nights before. It was warm but I still wore a jacket as I felt it made me look broader in the shoulders and it also looked a bit different. Eventually I came to the clearing, I could see the boating lake and the boathouse from about 200 yards away. To go to the boathouse where we had arranged to meet I had to cross a grassy bank. There was no sign of Ivan, Lennon and the rest of them so I decided to pause for a rest on the bank, as the boathouse was in sight. I laid my bike down on the grass and stretched myself out. I was there for about ten minutes when I heard the sound of voices; I looked up and saw their bikes. There was John Lennon, Pete Shotton, Nigel Whalley and Ivan Vaughan.

- *"Hey, steady on,"* I said, *"I was enjoying some peace and quiet."*

- *"Hi there Len,"* said Ivy, *"sorry we're a bit late but we had to wait for John, he had to mow the lawn at Mendips."*

Apparently this was a chore John regularly had to perform and the lawn in those days at Mendips stretched from the front of the house, around the side (now concrete) and right around the back.

- *"We gave him a hand,"* continued Ivan.

— 'The bank' in Calderstones Park - the gangs favourite haunt. —

They all parked their bikes in a heap on the bank beside mine and sprawled out. John pulled out a pack of Senior Service cigarettes, lit one and then gave one to Pete (Ivan and Nigel didn't smoke). Pete Shotton was wearing a blue style anorak and John a stone coloured one similar to the one that I had left at home.

- *"Like your jacket Len."* he said. I didn't know whether he was being serious or taking the piss but I still glowed at the compliment.

- *"Thanks but it's not mine I had to borrow it from my brother Wal. I've got one almost identical to the one your wearing at home."*

When I mentioned my brother's name Lennon broke into a giggle.

- *"Walter, Walter, lead me to the altar."* he mocked. *"That's an unusual name."*

he added.

- *"Yeah and we know someone else with an unusual name don't we?"* said Pete with a smile.

- *"No you don't Shotton, just keep your mouth shut or I'll shut it for you!"* Lennon's smile had disintegrated at Shotton's remark.

I only realised later that John's middle name was Winston and he was extremely secretive about anyone knowing it. We talked about music; I went through a list of singers that I liked at the time and as I did so Lennon made a comment about each one, as though he were judging a newly released pop record;

- *"Frankie Lane...Yeah I like Frankie Lane. But not as much as Shotton, you like Frankie don't you Pete?"*

- *"Oh yeah, he's one of my favourite singers, 'Cool Water' is brilliant."* replied Pete.

- *"Johnny Wray,"* I continued, *"I don't do a bad impression of Johnnie."*

- *"Yeah, he's okay but he looks a bit strange with that hearing aid."* Said John.

- *"Bill Haley - I like 'Rock Around the Clock' but I don't take to Bill Haley himself, more of a Billy Bunter than a pop star."* (Billy Bunter was a rotund comic character who was always eating).

The conversation carried on and it seemed to be only myself and John Lennon that were really interested in music.

- *"What about 'Sixteen Tons' by Teressa Ernie Ford?"*

Everyone started singing;

"Some people say a man is made of our mind." etc. etc. with a sort of competition to see who could get the "deep notes".

On this occasion I think that I won the competition because I was used to doing impressions of Paul Robeson, another singer with a deep voice.

- *"Hey Lenny that was good, who else do you take off?*

- *"I told you, Frankie Laine, Johnnie Wray, Bing Crosby."*

- *"Bing Crosby?"* Lennon laughed, *"who the bloody hell is Bing Crosby?"*

He knew full well who he was but mentioning the likes of Bing Crosby was unfashionable amongst youngsters with a rebellious streak. His was the voice of respectable, boring people. It was then that I realised that John Lennon was impressed with anyone who broke ranks, who was different, who would challenge what was accepted. I was going to mention how I liked listening to the Ink Spots when I was younger but I hesitated, trying to judge what reaction Lennon was going to give. Already we were looking to Lennon as a type of authority on what was good or bad in popular music but on this occasion I had misjudged the man. I plucked up the courage.

- *"Well I like the Ink Spots,"* I blurted out.

- *"Ah yeah, they are one of my favourite groups. What songs do you like Len?"*

- *"Whispering Grass."*

- *"Oh yeah I think that's great."*

I felt an instant bonding with this character Lennon. Then our conversation turned to our favourite film stars. We agreed on Bridget Bardot, as the sexiest woman on screen together with Gina Lollobrigida, with a particular "Yeah, Yeah" from Pete Shotton.
Marlon Brando, James Dean, were all our joint favourites. I had so much in common with this gang that I suddenly felt as though I had been accepted in.

- *"What shall we do now?"* asked Ivan, who had been relatively quiet and was seemingly bored with the way the conversation was going. *"Lets go on the rowing boats."*

We all agreed that it was such a lovely day it would be good to get close to the water.

- *"That's if Fred the boat keeper will let us on again."* suggested John. *"Remember last time we nearly sunk one of the boats."*

- *"Well Len can order the boat, he won't know Len."* said Pete *"We'll hide and then when he's hired it we'll all jump on."*

We all sauntered over to the boathouse where we had originally arranged to meet. I ordered a boat while the others hid behind the boathouse.

— Calderstones Park boating lake where the gang rowed. —

- *"On your own lad?"* asked Fred the boatman.

- *"Yeah, someone didn't turn up."* I replied as I clambered into the boat.

The suddenly, appearing from nowhere, the four lads ran to the edge of the jetty and jumped in before the boatman could do anything.

- *"Quick Len, get rowing or he'll catch us."* shouted John.

About half way around the lake John suddenly jumped up and did a Long John Silver impersonation.

- *"Ooh Arrh me lad, shiver me timbers. I can see the enemy approaching,"* and he went as if to stand on one leg in the boat to complete his impression.

However Pete managed to dissuade him as it would almost certainly have collapsed the boat. We were now entering a very narrow channel which was fortunately hidden from the view of the boatman Fred, as he would probably be waiting for us with the local park keeper by now, or "Parky Man" as we called him.

- *"Listen lads,"* I said, still rowing but getting pretty nervous at the thought of docking the boat knowing the reception we were going to get, *"we'll have to abandon the boat here, no one can see us and then we'll make off over the railings."* (The railings that surrounded the lake).

— Calderstones Park: Narrow boating lake channel where gang had races. —

We did this successfully and fortunately our bicycles were out of sight behind the part of the shed that bordered the main part of the park and we made our escape.

- *"Phew, that was great,"* said John.

- *"Yeah but we'll never be able to get on one of those again."* commented Pete.

Nigel Whalley by this time was gasping for breath as we cycled out of the park up towards Menlove Avenue, as he suffered bad asthma attacks. So we stopped while he breathed on his inhaler.

- *"Come on Nige, we can't stop now."* said Pete.

We arrived at the top of Yew Tree Road which joins onto Menlove Avenue. This was where I had to separate from the rest of the gang. We agreed to meet the next day "on the bank" at approximately the same time. I rode home feeling quite excited knowing that I had found a bunch of pals I could have fun with. I was looking forward to our next meeting.

The next day (Tuesday), although fine, was not as sunny as I made my way to meet the others at "the bank". By the time I got there, I could only see two bicycles and two people sprawled out beside them. As I approached I could only see Ivan Vaughan and John Lennon. Where were the others? I wondered as I approached.

- *"Hi John, hi Ivy. Where's Pete and Nigel?"*

- *"Hi Len,"* said John, *"Pete has to do some chores and Nigel's not very well. But we're here. What shall we do?"*

- *"Well,"* I said, *"I think we should give the park a rest for a couple of days after what happened yesterday. Do you know anywhere else we can go?"*

- *"Yeah I know a place. Lets go to Reynolds Park in Woolton."*

- *"Okay."* I said, and followed them on my bike.

John was wearing black tight bottomed trousers, a check shirt and a check tweed jacket. We were both wearing slip-on shoes. Slip-on shoes without laces were much more convenient to wear as you could slip them on and off easily. Ivan was dressed in a far more conventional manner.

Reynolds Park was situated at the top of Church Road, on the same road as the St Peter's Church. We arrived at the park at about 2:30p.m. We had no idea what we were going to do at the park but I think that secretly John and I were hoping that we might meet some girls. Anyway, as far as I was concerned it meant a new place and a change of scenery. We explored a bit, strolling around, went to the rose garden then sat down to have a cigarette.

- *"Hey John look at those two."* I said as I spotted two girls sitting on a bench.

- *"Yeah, which one am I supposed to look at?"* John replied disdainfully.

- *"The one with the pony tail."* I said.

- *"Oh yeah. She looks okay from here but what about the other one. She only looks about twelve years old. Anyway I bet that if you got up close the pretty one would have pimples all over her face."*

I lost interest at that remark and we spent some time talking about the rowing incident the day before. Ivan Vaughan by this time said that he had to go home as he had a lot of Greek homework to catch up on and so made his farewells. I was left with John Lennon.

By this time the two girls had wondered off down to the other end of the park that backed on to Beaconsfield Road. We decided to get a closer look, just to see what they were really like, so we followed them wheeling our bikes alongside us.

- *"Where the heck are they going, I don't know this part of the park."* said John, who had frequented the park on several occasions in the past.

We followed them from a reasonable distance. Eventually we came across an area that was surrounded by a huge stone wall with an open timber gate set into the middle of it. It was a very secluded part of the park, almost as though we had wandered into private property and the two girls had disappeared. We parked our bikes up against the wall and went through the gate. We entered a clearing that was covered in tall grass, interspersed with large trees. The whole area sloped downwards like an amphitheatre, towards the entrance of a dark tunnel within a wall which must only have been about five foot in height.

- *"I bet those girls have gone in the tunnel."* I said to John.

— Reynolds Park: The tunnel where Lennon, Len and Barbara Baker met. —

- *"Yeah, lets wait for them to come out."*

We waited for about a quarter of an hour and eventually we heard female voices and two girls appeared. Now they were closer we could see what they were really like.

- *"Hey Len - the tall one looks okay, the one with the pony tail, but I'm not so sure about the other one."*

The other girl was much smaller and did have a few pimples.

- *"What's your name?"* I asked the taller one of the two, who on closer inspection was actually quite attractive.

- *"My name's Barbara and this is Miranda, what's yours? What happened to the other lad that was with you?"*

- *"Oh you mean Ivan, well he studies a lot so he's gone home to do some work."*

- *"Does that mean that you don't study a lot?"* asked Barbara.

- *"We study what we feel like studying, I've got no time for all that school stuff."* replied John.

- *"What's your name?"* said Barbara, asking the question directly to me.

- *"My names Len, I'm 14."* I answered quickly, bumping up my age by a year to be on the same level as John, and added, *"what were you doing down that tunnel? It looks as though there might be rats in there."*

- *"We were just bored so we thought we would explore. We've never been down this end of the park before, even though we come here quite a lot."* replied Miranda.

- *"We generally hang out at Calderstones Park but we thought we'd come here for a change. There's usually about six of us but they're all doing other things today."* Said John.

John, in spite of me lying about my age, to his credit, did not let me down. He must have thought; okay we'll start on level terms, now let's see who can get Barbara first!

- *"Where do you live?"* I asked Barbara, who by this time showed us her very

pretty smile and white, even teeth.
- *"I live in Ridgetor Road, off Linkstor."*

- *"Oh, that's not far away from me, I think I've seen you before, don't you ride a bike?"* John asked.

- *"Yeah, I do have a bike and sometimes I go with some friends to play tennis in Calderstones Park."*

- *"That's where I've seen you before,"* nodded John. *"I think Len and I will go and explore the tunnel."*

- *"Hang on John. I've got a better idea. Why don't we let Barbara show us the tunnel and we can take it in turns who goes first. How do you feel about that Babs?"*

- *"Yeah okay, you'd better toss a coin to see who goes first."*

With that John Lennon quickly produced a three penny bit and tossed it up. I called heads and won. Barbara and I entered the tunnel.

- *"Phew it is dark in here, quick Babs give me your hand."*

- *"Don't call me Babs, I don't like it,"* she said, grasping my hand as we shuffled along.

We eventually reached half way and it was virtually pitch black but we could see just a glimmer of light. I could hear a shout, it was John;

- *"Hey are you alright in there?"*

Barbara and I ignored Lennon's question as by this time we were kissing quite passionately.

- *"Barbara,"* I said after about ten minutes, *"tell me honestly who you like best."*

- *"Why you of course."*

- *"Why's that?"*

- *"Because I like tall men."* Barbara replied.

After a while we vacated the tunnel and it was John's turn to go in. Meanwhile

Barbara's friend Miranda stayed behind, so while the other two left I chatted to Miranda, trying to find out a few more details about Barbara.

- *"So, how old is she?"*

- *"Oh she's fourteen, nearly fifteen. She's not really a great friend of mine, she just uses me for company when her other school friends are not available."*

- *"That's like being used, and yet your willing to wait for her, even though she's getting all the attention? I think she's very lucky to know you."*

Although Miranda was not attractive to me physically she was suddenly attractive to me as a personality, one thing I admired in a person was loyalty. Barbara and John then reappeared from the tunnel. John and I got together and discussed the situation.

- *"John, did you ask her who she liked best?"*

- *"Yeah and she said she fancied you - you dirty rat!"*

- *"Look John, I'm going to ask her out to be my steady girlfriend, if it doesn't work out you can step in, okay?"*

- *"Yeah Len, that sounds like a reasonable deal."*

I could see from John's face that his ego had been somewhat deflated, but I also felt a little as though I had cheated on him because I had lied to Barbara about my age. We walked with the girls out of the park into Church Road.

- *"Barbara, I'll meet you this Friday at the bottom of Linkstor Road where it joins Vale Road, at about 7:30? We could go for a bike ride, how does that suit you?"*

Barbara seemed taken aback by this decisive manner but she agreed. John and I parted after arranging to meet on "the bank" as usual and went to our respective homes for tea.

As I rode home I couldn't help whistling with joy at the exciting time that I was having this summer. New friends, my first real girlfriend and there were still about five weeks of holiday time left! I arrived back home just after 5 p.m.

- *"Mum,"* I called, as I flung my jacket over the banister, *"what's for tea?"*

Mum appeared from the kitchen.

- *"Len, that's all you ever say when you come in. You never tell me where you've been or what you've been doing. I feel as though I'm just taken for granted in this house. Your father when he gets up at 2:00 in the afternoon won't eat the meal I put before him. I feel like packing my bags and leaving!"*

- *"Ahh eh Mum, don't be silly. You know how much we love you. We get on alright don't we? We may not show it very often but we do appreciate you."*

- *"I know Len, I'm just a bit down. Are you out tonight?"*

I never told Mum that I had just met a girl. We didn't always discuss things like that in our house. It was left to me to learn the facts of life, through friends, books or films.

We spent a quiet evening together.

"The gang" and I spent the rest of the week on "the bank", meeting at the same time each day. Sometimes we would just lie there in the sun, our bicycles strewn about in an untidy heap. We would wrestle, crack jokes, impersonate famous singers of the day and watch the world go by from our vantage point on the sloping ground.

- *"Hey Pete did you know that Len managed to find himself a steady girl-friend?"* John asked as he lay stretched out on the grass.

- *"No - I didn't know that. You're a secretive sort Garry. When did this hap-pen?"*

- *"Oh just the other day. You weren't around so Ivan, John and I went to Reynolds Park and we met two girls. One of them was a peach and I asked her out."* I said gloatingly.

- *"So she chose you instead of John? What have you got that John hasn't?"*

- *"Oh charm, personality, looks...The list is endless."*

With that John Lennon got up and held me down on the grass, not in a vicious way but I could see the hurt look on his face, Pete joined in and they both held me down. This was like a red flag to a bull, I hated being trapped. In one super-human heave I threw them both off me.

- *"Don't ever do that to me again!"* I shouted, angry and red faced.

They got the message and we were all friends again. In fact so friendly that Lennon rested his head on my stomach and Pete Shotton rested his on Lennon's. It seemed as though nothing could separate the bond that we had formed.

Friday evening came around slowly for me as I was looking forward to seeing Barbara again. I arrived at the corner of Linkstor Road, not far from Pete Shotton's house to wait for Barbara. I wore my brown corduroy jacket, white shirt with a bright yellow tie. She arrived suddenly on her bicycle.

- *"Where did you say we'd go Len?"* she asked.

- *"I didn't say where, but lets go out to Haleshore, it's a lovely evening and we could watch the sunset over the Mersey estuary."*

- *"That sounds great, you lead the way."*

Haleshore was situated about six miles outside of Liverpool and was a well known beauty spot. We set off but I soon realised that I was not as fit as I had thought because Barbara quite often had to wait for me to catch up. We spent a pleasant romantic evening on the shore watching the sun go down and arrived back at the house at about 11p.m.

- *"Can I see you again?"*

- *"If you want to. Shall we go for a ride again somewhere?"* replied Barbara.

- *"Yeah, I'll think of somewhere else, not as far this time."*

We parted with a goodnight kiss and arranged to meet the following Friday. I wanted to ask her to go to the pictures but was reluctant because it would be difficult to get the money together for such a venture, so I settled for a bicycle ride again.

I paused before cycling back home, outside Pete Shotton's window and began whistling "Gee but it's great after bein' out late. Walkin' my baby back home". Pete recently recalled the incident to me;

"You were intent on making the most of the fact that you were the only one in the gang that had a steady girlfriend. It used to drive me mad. Your whistling was a sign of what a wonderful time you had had that night."

Often on my dates with Barbara, I would meet her as usual at the bottom of Linkstor Road, and there would be at least four members of the gang waiting with me to see Barbara arrive. I think she enjoyed all this interest from the lads and in particular from John Lennon. I used to notice the way that she would catch John's eye and he would catch hers. I thought then that my association with Barbara would not last for long. During the following weeks my assessment of the situation proved to be correct and eventually John started to go out with Barbara, with no opposition from me. I had a very "what will be will be" sort of attitude to these things. The meetings in the park continued as the summer progressed.

- *"Pete where do you keep getting all these cigarettes from?"* I asked Pete one day as he handed the ciggies around.

- *"Never you mind. I've got a job doing the papers. Anyway, it's none of your business."*

- *"I bet he's nicked them."* said John. *"Yeah, that's it isn't it Shotty? You've nicked them! You don't earn enough on your round to buy half a dozen packets of cigarettes."*

We decided to let it drop because Pete was about to walk off, taking his ciggies with him.

- *"Never mind,"* I said, *"it doesn't matter where he got them from, we're enjoying the benefits. Lets leave it at that."*

That afternoon there was only myself, John Lennon and Pete Shotton on the bank. Our trusty (or was it rusty) steeds lying by our sides, when from our vantage point John suddenly sat up. He then picked up a stick and began doing a Horatio Nelson impression, putting the stick to his eye as if it were a telescope.

- *"Heave to me hearties, I see fair maidens just off the starboard bow."*

We all sat up instantly, sure enough three maidens, wheeling their bicycles were traversing the park. John reached for his mouth organ, which he constantly carried with him, and started playing, desperately wanting to attract their attention.

- *"Well, well, well,"* I said, *"one for each of us. Who's going to do the fishing?"* (Keeping the nautical theme).

The two of them automatically turned to me and I got the message.

- *"Okay, I'll do the talking. You just keep playing that mouth organ, it sounds great. In fact I can see them looking over this way. I'll have to strike now."*

And with that I sauntered over looking as "cool" as possible but finding it very difficult as I did not have the bicycle with me and I usually used it as a prop or support. As I got within hailing distance I shouted;

- *"Hi there, would you like to listen to the great John Lennon? He is about to give a recital on his mouth organ."*

They looked at one another, giggled and changed their direction to walk over to the bank where John was still playing. Now all six of us were sitting on the bank - the fish had been caught. John, meanwhile continued with such songs as "Walkin my Baby Home", "Danny Boy" and "Swanee River". The girls seemed intrigued.

- *"I'm Len, that's John on the mouth organ and that's Pete."*

- *"My name's Maureen - people call me 'Mo', that's Kit and that's Mary."*

- *"Is this what you do all day?"* asked Kit.

John looked around as if to ask us.

- *"Yeah I think so. Not much else to do, unless of course you have something else in mind."* He said cheekily.

- *"I'm sick of this place, why don't we all go off for a ride somewhere, we've all got our bikes."* suggested Pete.

- *"You're sick of this place! I'll have you know that this place is hallowed ground. This is our second home. I love this place."* retorted John who had mis-interpreted what Pete had said.

- *"Yeah I agree, this place has become like a second home to me."* I said in agreement. There was a large element of truth in this statement of mine.

The girls looked on in amazement.

- *"I suppose you're all at school?"* asked Mo.

- *"That's a keen observation, how did you figure that one out?"* snapped John, who could not stand condescending remarks of any kind.

At this remark I could see that these two were immediately attracted to one another. Out of the other two there was only one that I could possibly find some feeling for and that was Kit.

- *"Come on fellahs,"* said Mo, *"it will do you good to get a bit of exercise."*

After a lot of murmuring and play acting, with John pretending to suddenly have cramp in his legs, the six of us picked up our bicycles and wandered out of the middle gate that led up Yew Tree Road. Directly opposite the gate was a narrow path that led up to Allerton Golf Links. The six of us stood outside the gate discussing where to go.

- *"What about going for a game of putting?"* I suggested, *"it's only just up the pathway and it costs about 2p for 9 holes."*

I could see that John was shaking his head secretly as I made this suggestion, he obviously wanted to do something other than play with golf balls. Pete Shotton made a similar gesture and I got the message. There seemed to be no takers for the putting green.

- *"Let's just get on our bikes and see where we end up. I know, lets ride out to Allerton Towers, it's not very far from here."* I suggested as an alternative.

There was no objection to this and so we cycled to Allerton Towers, which was just on the edge of Allerton Golf Links, about a mile away from Calderstones Park. I paired off with Kit, John with "Mo" and Pete with Mary. We found a grassy bank similar to that at Calderstones.

- *"Hey let's park our bikes here."* said John.

- *"Why do we always seem to end up on a hilly bank? It's strange, as though we're all used to a particular habitat,"* I observed. There was a great cluster of rhododendron bushes in the area.

- *"Yeah,"* said Lennon, *"that's because we like to be on top of things."*

We all saw the hint at a joke and laughed along with him.

I was "getting to know" Kit and I happened to look up; there was John Lennon lying on the grass with "Mo" in a sweet embrace, similarly engaged not far away were Pete Shotton and Mary and we had all formed a type of circle. Suddenly I felt a tug on my shirt, *"Hey what are you doing?"* I asked. Kit had started to pull my shirt out of my trousers at the stomach line. *"Ooh eh, you've got nice stomach muscles"*. she said, and quickly withdrew her hand. Needless to say we spent an enjoyable afternoon in their company. I don't believe we arranged to continue our association with the girls, although I was to bump into Maureen later on that summer.

Although I was having a great time with my new found friends I couldn't understand their general lack of interest in sport, ball games in particular. John Lennon's sporting activity it seemed was limited to an occasional visit to the Woolton Baths, as he was a good swimmer. I never offered to go along because I couldn't swim but I did miss playing cricket and football. Pete Shotton, for some unknown reason, was a Sunderland supporter (Sunderland was a town in the North East of England), perhaps because they had a great footballing tradition having been one of the first teams to form a football league. Nigel Whalley had by this time started to take an interest in golf and would play the odd round at Allerton Golf Links. Ivan Vaughan had no great sporting ability but was a very good swimmer. As a result "the gang" never played any ball games in Calderstones Park. I heard later from Pete Shotton that the reason for Lennon's apparent disinterest in ball games was that "he couldn't see properly without his glasses and always felt self conscious about wearing them".

Sometimes we did vary our activity and "stray away from home" - from the grassy bank! Sometimes we ventured as far as Allerton putting green, which was linked to Allerton Golf Club. One day we all decided to leave our bicycles at Ivan Vaughan's place and go across the Golf Links. Directly opposite Mendips was a path that led across the links to the putting greens. That day Pete Shotton had a tennis ball with him.

- *"Pete, what are you doing with that ball. You're not thinking of starting to play tennis are you?"* asked John

- *"Nah, but I wouldn't mind having a go."* said Pete.

We finally came across a disused building that had a very large roof that came down almost to eye level. Pete suddenly threw the ball up on the roof. It came back down again. I hit it back up using the palm of my hand. The game even appealed to John Lennon who by this time had put his spectacles on.

- *"Hey, even John's having a go!"* I remarked.

He turned to me with a sneer and slammed the ball high onto the roof.

- *"Get that then Len."* he said.

Roofball had been invented. It gradually became a pleasant diversion playing, "roofball" and everyone in the gang seemed to enjoy it. We were constantly looking for ways to have fun.

— Allerton Golf Course: The roof of this building was used by the gang for 'roofball'. —

One day in Calderstones Park we found ourselves watching the "old timers" playing bowls. The bowling Green was situated to the right of the Calderstones' entrance.

- *"Let's see if we can get a game."* suggested Pete.

- *"Yeah I'm game, "* said John and I agreed.

- *"I doubt very much whether they'll let us go on,"* said Ivan, *"they're mostly old men, you don't see any teenagers playing bowls. It's an old man's game."*

- *"Ah but we're not intending to play the old man's type of version. I can see there is some good fun to be had in there if we can get hold of a set of bowls."* retorted John. *"Who looks like the oldest and most respectable among us?"*

We all agreed that Pete Shotton fitted the bill most accurately, so Pete was sent to inquire after a set.

- *"How old are you?"* asked the attendant.

— Calderstones Bowling Green where the gang used to play. —

- *"Oh sixteen, I've just left school,"* lied Pete.

- *"Well okay, but you'll need two sets if you're friends are going to play."*

To our great surprise there seemed to be no great objection as Pete dutifully paid the bowling fee of about two shillings, which he collected bit by bit from us.
- *"What the hell is this for?"* asked John, who was inspecting the circular rubber mat in his hand.

- *"It's for putting your feet on as you stoop down to bowl in order to protect the grass."* I answered knowingly, as I had already played bowls with my father.

- *"Nah, I can't see it, look that old geezer is throwing it all over the place - like this...."* With that John threw the black mat and just missed one of the bowls that was being played across the green.

I made my apologies for John, saying that he was from a special school and didn't realize what he was doing. The explanation was not only accepted but the dear old man also gave us some instructions on how to play bowls, he must have thought that we were all from the same special school. Our "bowling" techniques then created havoc, as we had virtually been given a licence to do as we liked.

- *"Hey lets see if I can knock the bowls as the old geezer's are throwing theirs."* suggested John.

The bowls from the elderly gentleman traversed the green. We would let fly our bowls and thus we spent a hilarious afternoon, often knocking out their bowls in mid flight, completely ruining their game. This is another place that we're going to get barred from, I thought. First the boating lake, now the bowling green, what next? I wondered.

—Calderstones House: In the 50's the building was a café that the gang frequented.—

On Friday and Saturday evenings the park would be overflowing with teenagers congregating on the grassy area immediately opposite the café as it was then (the mansion house and offices as it is now). The vast majority of them had bicycles, the lads with their smart racing cycles proudly wearing the latest riding gear, without helmets of course, as they had not been introduced as a safety measure yet. The "gang" would observe them from our outpost on the bank, never joining in - we were quite happy to be separate from the masses.

- *"Hey here comes the Lone Ranger - where's Tonto I wonder?"* said John as we watched a chap strut across the park.

His bicycle had about fifteen gears. It was a racing lightweight and obviously his pride and joy. He was holding the bicycles drop handlebars by the central pivot ever so lightly, as if to say, "look everyone my bike is so great that it almost doesn't need any help from me, it can almost run by itself".

- *"I don't know who he thinks he is but talk about a poser! Where did he get all the money to pay for a machine like that anyway?"* Said Pete.

- *"He probably does a paper round around the whole of Liverpool."*

- *"Very funny Len, can't you do better than that?"* I ignored John's remark.

- *"That's Ego Evans from Quarry, don't let him hear you talking about him for Pete's sake. He does weight lifting and things like that, I wouldn't want to rumble with that geezer."* Said Pete.

- *"Anyway, who would want to have a bike with ten or fifteen gears. I've already got enough with five,"* remarked John, *"you'd never even be in a position to be able to use the fifteenth gear around the streets of Liverpool. It's all for show. I hate show offs."*

- *"Hey you can talk Lennon, you do a bit of that yourself."*

- *"What do you mean by that Shotton? Come on, out with it."*

- *"Well...."*

- *"Come on Shotton."*

Pete was hesitating now.

- *"Well, you've got a walk similar to Ego Evans - just like a strutting peacock."*

By this time Pete Shotton had moved away from John, half expecting retaliation for this remark. John was quiet for a moment, well aware that Pete was waiting for him to react violently. However, John answered quietly;

- *"Do you know Shotty, you're dead right. But Ego Evans copied it from me!"*

Typical of John to have the last word. We watched as Ego Evans disappeared and was swallowed up by the assembled crowd of teenagers. Someone came up to him and started to admire his machine.

- *"Hey, look out. Here comes the weirdo."* I said and everyone looked to see which direction I was looking in.

- *"Hey, so it is,"* said John, *"let's pretend that we're asleep then he might go away."*

- *"I don't fancy lying down with my eyes shut with that fellah around."* I said. *"He might jump on you."*

- *"Len, I know he might look like a homo"* (slang word for homosexual), *"but he's not going to take a jump on you while the rest of us are here is he? These people like to get you on your own. No I reckon he's harmless. Sh sh he's seen us, he's coming over. Let's have a laugh!"*

I will call this character Sam, as his real name has escaped my memory, although the leering face has stuck with me. Anyway I think that we called him Sam because we tended to call people by what we considered to be a good name for them rather than by their actual names. Here was an instance of this. The sun was quickly disappearing beyond the trees on the park lake, and apart from the occasional solitary person walking their dog everyone was concentrated on the area in front of the café, apart from us that is.

Sam by this time was leering down at us. Suddenly Lennon as if struck by a thunderbolt gets up like a rabbit out of a burrow.

"Ooh, aah, shit - ooh. Cor you frightened the life out of me with that horrible face. I thought I was having a nightmare and I wasn't. It's real, it's not a Boris Karlof movie - why it's Sam. Phew what a relief." Then after a short pause politely said; *"Hi Sam, how are you doin'. "*

Now we had bumped into Sam on various occasions while we were in the park and he knew what we were like, although we took the piss he usually took it in a light hearted way. It was just as well because the poor man suffered a terrible amount of abuse and piss taking from us all, but in particular from John Lennon.

- *"Sam, where did you get that tan. Sam, Sam, where did you get that tan?"*

His face was swarthy and smooth. His mouth was thick and slimy. His teeth were white and false and he continuously shoved his dentures around his mouth with a clicking sound. He walked with a slightly bent back, had reasonably smart clothes but always kept his hands in his pockets. He was always on his own. These we decided were sufficient factors to point to his being a lecherous individual. The sort who took little boys in the woods.

- *"Sam has anyone ever told you, you look a bit like John Wayne the film star, well I mean you've got a similar hair style; all greased back, what do you use to keep it down? Lard?"* Lennon remarked. Sam ignored the insult and enquired;

- *"Why is it that whenever I see you lads you're always in this spot and you never seem to be with any one else?"*

- *"That's because firstly; we like each other and secondly; we don't like anyone else!"* Was the quick reply from John who was enjoying himself at Sam's expense. *"Come to think of it Sam, we never see you with anyone else, haven't you got a girlfriend or a wife?"*

Sam then gave us a "sob story" about his wife dying a few years ago and how his children had emigrated long ago, leaving him all on his own. We didn't give him much sympathy and he soon loped off, no doubt regretting his intrusion into the closely knit little group. The park closing hours were on the signpost as being an hour after sunset, at this rate we only had about half an hour to vacate the park. Teenagers were beginning to band together and migrate towards the exit as most were going in the same sort of direction home.

- *"What shall we do now?"* I asked.

- *"I'm getting bored and it's starting to get cold. Has anyone got any money to get some chips? Let's follow that gang, I think that they are going towards the "chippy" in Penny Lane."*

No one disagreed, someone had about a shilling, this would buy three bags of chips at 4p a bag. The three of us; John Lennon, Pete Shotton and myself followed the rest of the group, not really mixing with them as we made our way towards the Four Season's exit of Calderstones Park that led onto Green Lane.

We were about 300 yards down Menlove Avenue, going into Allerton Road, past the Penny Lane roundabout and towards the fish and chip shop when I recognized the girl that Lennon had "gone with" at Allerton Towers. It was "Mo", Lennon and Shotton were ahead of me by this time and I dropped back to chat to her.

- *"Hey remember us?"* I asked. *"John's over there with Pete."*

- *"Of course, it's Len isn't it? You don't usually come with us to the chippy."*
- *"No we don't, but John was feeling hungry and it's not often we have the spare*

cash to buy fish and chips these days. By the way, do you still see Kit?"

We were walking along past some seats and as we were talking had slowed down and had become separated from the rest of the crowd.

- *"Hey Mo, lets sit down here for a while. We can catch up with the rest later."*

To my surprise she agreed and we sat down and chatted for a while but eventually ended up having a "necking session" (kissing) on the park bench. By the time our little session had finished the crowd were well on their way down Menlove Avenue and so we hopped on our bikes and caught up with the rest.

I never saw Maureen again - I think she had a steady boyfriend at the time. It has always remained a puzzle for me why she decided to stay behind that summer's evening and why, when she had the opportunity of meeting up with John Lennon again she didn't seem to have been that bothered. Perhaps John Lennon was not every girls "cup of tea" after all! I believe in retrospect that these situations are just assurances to boost our confidence and raise our self esteem. A re-assurance that we are desired and that there are those that are ready to satisfy our need for affection.

4

Musical Influences on the Quarrymen:

Why Skiffle became a craze in the United Kingdom and especially in Liverpool-

It would be easy to say that Skiffle music became popular because of it's amateurish nature; you didn't have to read music in the formal sense and the instruments were fairly basic and home made. However, this would be an oversimplification.

The seeds of the popularity of skiffle music lay in a mixture of social and economic factors. Many people in 1950s England were beginning to experience the "I've never had it so good factor", (a phrase coined by the then contemporary conservative prime minister Harold MacMillan).

The Second World War had finally come to an end in 1945 and by the 1950s most of the hardships experienced in it's aftermath were receding and were replaced by new feelings of optimism. People generally felt that there would never be another war. That people had suffered immediately following the end of the war there was no doubt; the rationing of essential foodstuffs not only limited the quantity of a family's consumption but also prevented them from choosing their own *type* of lifestyle. Yet there was a general feeling that once the decade of the 1940's was over the 1950's would bring the dawn of a new era, people hoped for peace and stability; they could now begin to think more about how to spend their leisure time as the great national emergency was finally over.

Britain itself was beginning to prosper again. The city of Liverpool was still the second largest sea port in the U.K. Liners would stream constantly to America, maintaining the long history of cultural and economic exchange with the country that had so recently come to it's aid in an hour of extreme need.

During the 1950s it was a common sight to see foreign vessels docked in the river Mersey paying no more than courtesy visits.

On a Saturday night it was not unusual to see groups of sailors from the U.S.A., Norway, Sweden and Canada (among others) walking into town, visiting the pubs and restaurants looking for pretty girls. Young people in the city got to know the sailors and formed friendships, it was a method of cultural exchange and each enlightened the other on the things that were happening in their respective countries, in terms of fashion, music and standards of living. Communication and an exchange of ideas were taking place first hand.

The communications industry itself was developing at a very rapid rate. Ordinary people began to be able to afford televisions, record players, telephones etc. for the first time. Those American sailors who had record players on board ship would sometimes be able to invite Liverpool girls on board and play them the type of music that was emerging from the States. All these influences were soaked up by the youth of Liverpool as in all the other great sea ports. Liverpool was particularly receptive however, due to it's geographical links with America.

Liverpool people were a hybrid mixture of cultures themselves, namely Irish, Welsh and African. The wealth of Liverpool was made initially through the exploitation of the slave trade. It was therefore also from Liverpool that many African slaves were shipped to America to work on the cotton plantations, where Blues music first began.

All these factors helped contribute to the need for a method of expression for these newly found freedoms. The old Victorian values were being eroded, the idea that "the establishment" was the ultimate authority was being challenged by the youth culture that was itself changing and developing so fast.

The choices people faced as to how to spend their leisure time was expanding. There were now coffee bars available where teenagers could meet and chat. Previously there wasn't anywhere where young people could congregate except in pubs and those youths that were under age would be refused entry.

The early 50's music that was prevalent was all coming from America. It was the era of the ballads and jaunty popular songs. Songs made popular by the likes of Pat Boone, Guy Mitchell, Frankie Laine, and Johnny Wray were mainly love songs or ballads.

At around this time, the latter end of 1953 Elvis Presley was making his debut in a small recording studio in Memphis, recording a record for his mother's birthday. During 1954 and 1955 he had a hit record in the top 5 of the country music charts; "Baby Let's Play House."

It was also in 1955 that the film "Rock around the Clock" was released. The theme song by the same name was performed by Bill Haley and the Comets. As the theme song played, the pictures accompanying it were that of teenagers dancing down the aisles - the music seemed to have the effect of demanding a response from the audience.

Rock 'n' Roll was here to stay. The church, especially the more evangelical sections, believed that this new form of music was "bringing the animal instincts" out in young teenagers and they strongly condemned it.

Meanwhile, in the summer of 1955 a small group of teenagers were gradually coming under the effect of this music. They were in time to form the Quarrymen skiffle group and included the 15 year old John Lennon. There was a common thread that was running through the contemporary musical revolution - the pre-eminence of the guitar as the principal musical instrument. It became to the teenager almost a status symbol of whether you were "with it" or "just a square". "With it" meant you were following the fashion, with the new "Tony Curtis" styled haircut for the boys characterised by a "quiff" at the front.

To be able to play the guitar was considered by the boys in those days a way of attracting the opposite sex, at least that was the view from the masculine side, whether the females in the population were suitably impressed I have yet to find out. Those who had a guitar were therefore "with it".

The Origins of Skiffle -

The musical craze that hit Great Britain in the mid 1950s was called Skiffle.

The definition of the musical term "skiffle" as stated in the New Groves Dictionary of Music is that it refers to, "a type of entertainment that mostly black musicians performed at 'rent parties' in the Chicago districts of the U.S.A. in the 1920's." The main purpose of these parties was to earn money in order to pay rent. People would turn up with their own food, drink and home made musical instruments and improvise a mixture of blues, folk, gospel and jazz, mixed with the popular music of the time. The sound which emerged would depend upon who had attended and what kind of instruments they had brought with them.

I believe it is important to relate where the roots of skiffle started because without it's development and it's eventual commercialization by Lonnie Donnegan (who first brought it back to the U.K.), then there would have been no Quarrymen and consequently no Beatles. However, the whole process started with the Blues.

The blues began in the deep south of the USA at the time of the American Civil War. The "blues" was a word that summed up a feeling that the black slaves had because of their oppression under their white employers and the feelings that ventured forth from this state of mind. It came out as a groaning as if under a heavy burden and this grieving state had to be expressed in words. It was a heart-felt emotion and because of this it could not fail to have an effect on the emotion's of anyone who heard it. It was like a musical cry from the heart.

The blues grew into a particular style and the groaning was transmitted through the way the blues singer would play his guitar and the tone of his voice. The people who sang the blues were mainly black American slaves. They did not know a note of musical theory and usually could not read or write and so they had to make up the music and the words as they went along: it was this very spontaneity that proved to have such an effect on the listener. It came forth often as a type of prayer.

There are some similarities here to the Quarrymen. Although none of us were illiterate, not one of us could read a note of music and we therefore had to resort to improvisation. We were really imitating that which had already been passed down from previous musical generations: the inherited legacy of the blues. This is why it is so critically important because however talented a person or group of people are, the initial impetus has often come from those who have paved the way before.. This fundamental process can be traced in all aspects of life, not just in music.

The blues was first created by the black slaves as they worked on the cotton plantations, as this was the American South's main industry. The words (lyrics) that came forth were related to what they were experiencing in everyday life. There were also workers employed by the railroads and in the lumber camps and the tempo of the songs that came forth was dictated and related to the type of work they were undertaking. Thus a work song coming from a gang breaking up rocks would be related to the speed at which the sledgehammer was used as it was yielded in the slaves' hands.

The cotton plantations were dissolved following the Northern States victory in the Civil War and many of the work songs only continued amongst the black American workers who found employment running leased small holdings owned often by unscrupulous white landlords. These people were still in captivity (although legally free) therefore, and the blues continued to be performed.

The instruments involved in what was now developing into a pronounced 'blues style' were a transition from what their ancestors had played in Africa, such as the banja which developed in the United States as the banjo. The dominant employers would not allow the black workers to play drums as this in their mind was associated with tribal war dancing and it was thought it would provoke the workers to be disobedient. However stringed instruments were allowed and so the blues singer developed a skill in playing the banjo and guitar.

After the Civil War the southern states were re-organised and new boundaries drawn up. The white community meanwhile drew up oppressing segregation laws to keep the black man in his place and this caused more strife. Things hadn't changed much for the black people, they still weren't free. This gave the blues singer even more ammunition for declaring his grievance. Ballads were now being sung that would describe the exploits of their black heroes like John Henry.

Songs came forth such as Railroad Bill. These were the songs that Lonnie Donnegan took up and recorded in the skiffle heydays of the 1950's. 'See See Rider' was another of this type to be eventually adapted and recorded by Elvis Presley. Elvis always proclaimed that the blues had been a great influence on his style of singing.

Many of the performers of these work songs were employed by street sellers selling their 'wonder cures' and of course in their travels this helped to spread the 'blues' influence towards the northern states. There were also at the same time street evangelists singing their gospel songs which were not unlike the 'blues' in terms of their heartfelt conviction and sound.

Many skiffle songs came about therefore as a result of a combination of blues and gospel songs. Songs that came forth out of experiencing toil in the hot sun and gospel songs that yearned for a better life 'on the other side'. There was a common yearning for freedom running though both. Many of the songs had repetitive lyrics and took on the form of a chant.

For example

"Take this hammer and carry it to the Captain.
Tell him I'm gone, tell him I'm gone.
This is the hammer that killed John Henry.
But it won't kill me , but it won't kill me."

Because of it's repetition the listener could not fail to get the message and this also gave it a rhythmic style that would eventually be taken up by skiffle.

In the 1920's and into the 1930's the black workers searched for a better life and now that the northern states were opened up to them by the introduction of the railroad system many went north to find it. They would often hitch rides on the railroad cars. They moved to the large cities of Detroit and Chicago where man-ufacturing industries were being developed and growing quickly as the age of the automobile got under way. This led to more problems; because there was such an influx of black workers to these cities they found it difficult to obtain living accommodations at a reasonable price and rents were raised to exorbitant

— Pete Shotton and Len Garry with washboard and 'Tea chest bass' - May 1997 —

levels. Many of them were forced to live and sleep on the streets as a consequence. Some did find accommodation but because of the high rent they were
forced to sing for their rent money.

They held what was known as rent parties for the specific purpose of
raising enough money to pay the rent. It was as though they had left one fight
for survival to be faced with another.

However with all things there must be motivation and it was this practical fight for survival that gave birth to skiffle. Blues music remained and skiffle was a by-product. These black performers were poor by any standards. They
had no money to pay for instruments such as clarinets or trumpets and so they
looked for instruments that were no more common than household objects, anything that would make a different sound. Kitchen utensils were utilised such as
washboards washtubs and the like. The result was a skiffle group.

At the same time street bands were appearing in New Orleans. I suppose they
were the buskers of their day. These were called spasm bands and they would
use bottles, tin cans, and jugs and they would often accompany street traders or
go before them to rouse people's awareness of the oncoming demonstration.
This was skiffle in it's embryonic form.

The spasm bands of New Orleans, the bands of the Chicago suburbs were laying down the foundation for the skiffle, jazz and rock and roll movements for
generations to come. two particular instruments used were the washtub and the
washboard and these are of particular interest to me for obvious reasons. The
washtub bass would usually be made from an inverted steel wash tub and having looked at the way the American wash tub bass was constructed I perceived
that there were some advantages in it's design over the square box tea chest that
I played. There was however one major disadvantage.

The washtub would almost certainly have not fit into the under-stairs luggage
compartment of the Liverpool buses due to it's irregular shape. However
because it was made of steel it had a better resonance and therefore produced a
clearer sound. It was oval in shape and had steel handles on the side. The handles would be removed and a hole drilled through the center. From the hole a
piece of string or cat-gut was fixed and securely tied to the end of a wooden
pole. This pole was notched at the base so that it would fit securely onto the

rimmed edge of the up-turned tub. I used to find it difficult to keep the pole still on top of the square tea chest, although some skiffle groups used upturned cylindrical steel drums which had an edge to them similar to the tubs used in America.

There has been a suggestion that the term skiffle was a British invention and even the king of skiffle, Lonnie Donnegan, stated that there were no genuine recordings of it in the 1920's. In fact this was not so. An American blues singer called Charlie Spanel recorded "Hometown Skiffle" in 1929 and for this he employed all home-made instruments. At the same time the "South Happiness Street Society Skiffle Band" were performing in New Orleans (this would have been a difficult name to fit onto a tea chest).

The other instrument of interest to me and that we used in the Quarrymen was the washboard, played at the time by Pete Shotton.

The washboard, in the type of bands that I have just described, was sometimes fixed to a stand and the player would use steel thimbles, a piece of wire or some-times his own fingernails - anything that would make a scraping sound. In those days there were entire bands made up of just washboard players. One of note was the Clarence Williams Jug and Washboard Band.

Robert Brown, otherwise known as Washboard Sam, was perhaps the most famous washboard player. He often performed with Big Bill Broonzy and he would sing the blues as he played using thimbles on all his fingers.

The street bands of those days would also use instruments such as fry-ing pans, paper and comb, harmonica or clappers (bones). The sounds produced were primitive, earthy and encapsulated the work song feel that helped to reflect the life and experience of the American black man. It also helped to lay the foundations of rock and roll that would follow two decades later.

One of the first performers of skiffle as a group were the Mound City Blue Blowers led by Red McKenzie. They came from the United States and played in London in 1925. Red could not play any recognised instrument but resorted to playing the 'comb and paper'. They were affectionately known as the Blue Blowers.

This band, because they would resort to using practically anything that might create a different sound, were not taken seriously in London but found that they were better received in the working class areas of the north of England. I think this speaks for itself: the working class people who were generally struggling to make ends meet could identify with a band that 'made do' with using everyday household items and converting them to musical instruments.

In 1949 Ken Colyer formed the Crane River Jazz Band with a view to duplicating the sounds of the New Orleans Jazz that had flourished in the 1920's. IN 1952 Ken went to New Orleans and came back with blues and folk songs from this era. At the same time Chris Barber formed the New Orleans Jazz Band and Ken joined the Barber band in 1953. Also in the band was Lonnie Donnegan, playing banjo.

Chris and Ken soon split up to form their own bands and they both began to introduce skiffle songs in their repertoire. Chris Barber recorded "Everybody Love My Baby" and "Whoop It Up" in 1951.

His band on this recording was called The Washboard Wonders. This was probably the first recording of skiffle in the U.K. although it was Ken Colyer that really promoted skiffle in this country. In 1954 he included a number of skiffle songs on a jazz LP., one of them being "Midnight Special".

Chris Barber who was also dabbling into skiffle and recorded songs such as "Rock Island Line" and "John Henry" which were basically adaptations of the railroad work songs. Lonnie Donnegan was instrumental and main vocalist on the record that was an LP. that included more traditional style jazz numbers.

"Rock Island Line" was eventually released as a single and it went quickly into the top ten in 1956. At the same time "Heartbreak Hotel" by Elvis Presley had entered the top ten in the U.S.A. .

The greatest influence on Lonnie Donnegan was undoubtedly the black American singer Huddie 'Leadbelly' Ledbetter and it was he who originally recorded "Rock Island Line" "Bring A Little Water Sylvie", "Pick A Bale Of Cotton" all of which were to become hits for Lonnie Donnegan.

Because of Leadbelly's importance I think it is appropriate to include a small biography of the man.

Leadbelly was born in Louisiana in 1885. He started out as a musician at the age of fifteen and his songs came about while he would listen to the cotton pickers on the plantations. For instance the water carrier would be in constant demand by the workers toiling in the hot sun, the words uttered by the workers formed the basis of the song, "Bring a little water Sylvie, bring a little water now, bring a little water Sylvie, every little once in a while." This was recorded eventually by Lonnie Donnegan and became part of his skiffle repertoire.

Between the years 1920 - 1930 Leadbelly was sent to prison for two counts of attempted murder. The first time he was in prison for five years, then released, but was back again on a similar charge in 1930.

Leadbelly had learned to play the 12 string guitar and while in prison he composed a large number of songs. I suppose he was the first commercial blues singer/songwriter. He recorded "Rock Island Line" in 1942, fourteen years before Lonnie Donnegan's first success with the same song.

Lonnie Donnegan's success continued in the United States in 1956 having been booked to tour with Pat Boone and other famous American singing stars. Lonnie formed his own skiffle group when he returned to England after his first tour of the USA. He then toured the UK.

The skiffle band that Lonnie formed had developed in line-up and sound from the skiffle sounds of the 1920's generated by the jug-blowers, and the comb and paper players. The main instrument was now the guitar and this was emerging as the most versatile and popular instrument and was to change the sound and direction of popular music for generations to come.

There was another movement in the music scene also emanating from the USA. Following on from the success of "Rock Around The Clock" by Bill Haley, a new star emerged whose influence would have world-wide effect. His name was Elvis Aaron Presley. he also played guitar though his music was likened more to blues and rockabilly than skiffle and his record of "Heartbreak Hotel" reached number one in the USA in 1956. This particular man and his record had a tremendous impact and influence on John Lennon and his teenage friends in 1956.

Another major influence was Chuck Berry who was introducing a particular rhythmic style to blues songs which became known as rhythm and blues.

Meanwhile the skiffle craze continued in Britain and to some degree in America although there it had to compete with the emergence of rock and roll. The only American group that had a success in the UK at this time was Johnny Duncan and his Bluegrass Boys with "Last Train To San Fernando". It's success was due mainly because the buying public associated the bluegrass style of music with that of skiffle.

The skiffle sound was now becoming commercialised and the BBC set aside complete T.V. programmes for the skiffle loving public such as the Six Five special and the Saturday Skiffle Club.

Lonnie Donnegan's popularity was at it's peak in 1957. This was also the year that the Quarrymen Skiffle Group were starting to perform in public and many other skiffle groups formed in the major cities and towns all over the UK. Skiffle competitions were held and this attracted literally thousands of entries.

There were new skiffle groups apart from Lonnie Donnegan's that were becoming very popular. Groups such as 'Chas' McDevitt's Skiffle Group who had a hit with "Freight Train" featuring a female singer called Nancy Whiskey.

Lonnie Donnegan meanwhile after his second tour of the USA on 1957 was top of the bill at the London Palladium. Towards the latter end of 1957 skiffle had begun to lose it's basic sound. It became popular amongst ballad singers and even orchestras such as Ron Goodwin who had a hit with "Skiffling Strings".

It was inevitable that skiffle would soon be swallowed up in the wake of the oncoming rock and roll giant. Rock and roll was too powerful, combining everything from skiffle, blues and gospel leaving skiffle a skeleton of it's former self.

The Quarrymen, at this time, were overcome by rock and roll's impact and many of the skiffle songs were fast disappearing from our repertoire. The electric guitar was emerging with the oncoming rhythm and blues. New sounds were being developed and made possible by this electrification. Amplification and loud speakers and other pieces of new equipment were quickly becoming available to the new generation of 'rockers'.

By the end of 1957 skiffle had virtually died, however it was still at it's peak when a disused cellar in a Liverpool back street had been turned into a club by jazz fanatic Alan Sytner. It was to be named The Cavern Club. He was the son of a local doctor and was running two jazz clubs in Liverpool, one in the city centre. The city club became so popular that he looked for larger premises and he found the ideal spot in the depths of a disused warehouse in Matthew Street. On the 16th January 1957 the Cavern Club was officially opened.

5

Life up to the formation of the Quarrymen (including the enrollment at Quarry Bank by Len Garry and Billy Turner.)

It was during this wonderful summer of 1955, (see Chapter Three) that John Lennon was becoming aware of his musical talent, amidst all the mayhem and escapades of the "gang". He carried his harmonica with him wherever he went and often entertained us with his renderings of Frankie Laine's "Cool Water" and Johnnie Ray's "Little White Cloud". He had first been given a harmonica lesson by one of the students that his Aunt Mimi had taken in at Mendips when he was ten years old.

As far as I remember John's real enthusiasm was only stirred by the singers who conveyed a certain uniqueness of style or sound and within this area his range of musical tastes varied immensely. Now that he had his first steady girlfriend a certain romantic side of his nature was stirred by the singing of Julie London's "Cry me a River". She had a sultry texture to her voice that appealed to him. Eartha Kitt's "Old Fashioned Millionaire" and Peggy Lee's "Lady and the Tramp" were also on his favourites list.

The only opportunity we had for tuning in to what was happening in America were the few record playing programme's by the BBC such as "Family Favourites" a request programme that was on at Sunday lunch times. Then we

— Len Garry —

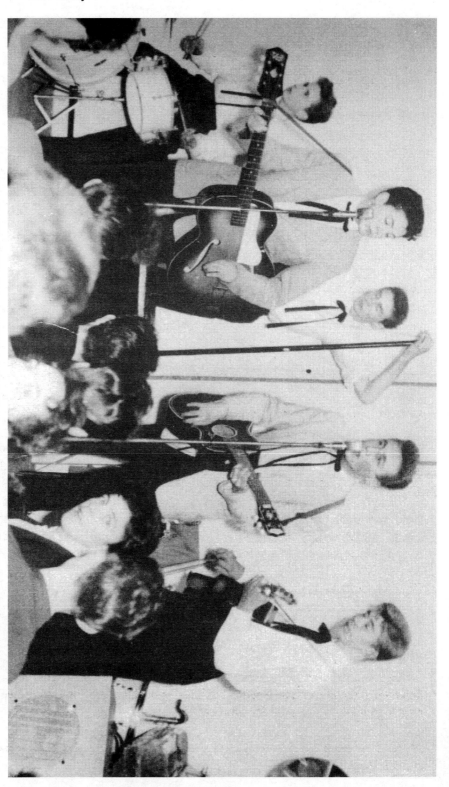

— Colin Hanton, Paul McCartney, Len Garry, John Lennon and Eric Griffiths 23rd November 1957 Clubmoor Hall —

discovered a new source. On the 208 medium wave band was Radio Luxembourg, a radio station that was independent from the BBC and funded by private advertising. All of us became regular listeners to the Jack Jackson Show, which played a lot of American Rock 'n' Roll music. John became hooked on such artists as Bill Haley, Chuck Berry and Gene Vincent, whose "Be Bopa Lula" became one of his firm favourites.

It is therefore important to state that John Lennon fell under the influence of the Rock 'n' Roll or rhythm and blues sounds of Elvis and all the previously mentioned artists and not the sounds of the skiffle movement that was taking place at the same time. Skiffle and the ability for people to access such music easily acted only as a catalyst and precursor to his continuing obsession for Rock 'n' Roll music. I felt a close affinity with John all the way through this developing process and our musical tastes remained almost identical.

Our summer holidays ended in the early part of September 1955 and we all went back to school for the autumn/winter term with heavy hearts. All of us had great stories to tell about our hilarious escapades. I meanwhile renewed my friendship with Billy Turner. During the latter months of 1955 I tried to knuckle down to some school work which I was finding increasingly hard to do.
I think that meeting new exciting friends who didn't seem to take their school days seriously had a "knock on" effect on me and I continuously looked for ways to relieve my boredom at school.

On Saturday mornings I usually went round to call on Bill at his house, deliberately making it early in the morning as we liked to listen to a children's request show on BBC radio called "Uncle Mac". We would listen to songs such as "Spanky the Talking Piano" - entirely children's music but mixed in with these would be bits that we enjoyed listening to such as "Rock Around the Clock" by Bill Haley and various other American artists like Pat Boone. My musical interests were still being fed.

One Saturday afternoon in late October Bill and I decided to go out and visit a certain small ice cream and coffee bar which according to Bill sold the most delicious ice creams. Having renewed our pocket money the night before we found ourselves, on a cold October afternoon, enjoying our even colder ice creams. The café was sectioned off into small booths, the front window was covered by a curtain which appeared to be made of knitting needles. Hence we nicknamed the place "The Needles". Sitting in the adjacent booth were two girls chatting and enjoying their ice creams.

- *"Hey Bill- there's a couple of girls in the next booth, lets ask them if we can sit with them."*

Bill pretended to go to the counter to ask for something in order to get a view of what they looked like. From his counter position he looked over at me and gave me the thumbs up sign which meant that they looked okay. Before long we had joined them and made our introductions. Bill and I had agreed before we set out that if we happened to meet some girls we would say that our age was 14 rather than 13. I still had the notion that the age of 14 was an acceptable age, particularly with girls, the same notion that I had earlier on in the year when I met Barbara Baker. Bill had no problem as he had already reached the age of 14.

The girls names were Margaret Jones and Beryl Woods. I took to Margaret who was dark haired and slim and Beryl looked tailor made for Bill, being a bit shorter and plumper.

- *"What do you do with yourselves in the evenings?"* I asked.

- *"Well I have a lot of homework to do most of the week but on Friday evenings Beryl and I go to the youth club that belongs to the church on the corner of Ullett Road."* Margaret replied.

- *"Oh yeah, what do you do there?"*

- *"Oh we have quizzes, sometimes country dancing and games. Why don't you two come along one night?"*

- *"What do you think Bill, shall we give it a try?"* I asked.

- *"Yeah, it sounds like a good idea. Listen girls, we'll meet you there next Saturday night."*

The girls agreed and we parted company. Billy and I walked slowly back up to Lance Lane, not the end of the lane that I lived in as I was still officially banned from seeing Bill. Lance Lane was split into two sections by Woolton Road, we arrived at the section that was adjacent to the Abbey Cinema. In high spirits we walked back to our homes. I was excited at the thought of having a new girl-friend, although I had not asked Margaret yet. It was just what I needed to boost my enthusiasm for life following the anti-climax of the summer that had gone by.

The following Friday Bill and I decided that we would only go to the youth club at closing time because although we fancied the girls who we'd met we didn't really fancy belonging to any church youth club, it wasn't our scene.

—The Abbey Cinema - was Lennon's supermarket - now Somerfields.—

We arrived about 10 p.m., just as it was closing. We spotted Margaret and Beryl as they were leaving the church hall.

- *"Hiya girls, I'm sorry we couldn't make it on time but Bill has a sick mother and we had to look after her."*

We were not afraid to paint ourselves as caring youngsters, we thought this might endear us into the hearts of the females we met. It appeared to work this time.

- *"Oh I'm sorry about your mother Billy, I do hope she gets better soon. I can understand why you two didn't turn up till now."* said Margaret in a sympathetic tone.

- *"Why don't we arrange to meet one day during the week. We could just go for a walk in the park or for a cup of coffee."* Beryl suggested.

We all agreed. The following months Billy and I were occupied seeing our two new girl friends.

One evening I received a phone call.

- *"Hello Childwall 2936?"*

- *"Hiya Len, it's Pete. Pete Shotton."*

- *"Cor Pete. I haven't heard from you for ages. How are you doing?"*

- *"I'm fine but bored to death. I miss those lazy summer days by the bank."*

- *"So do I Shotto. Listen, I've linked up with Billy Turner again and we've met these two girls. I've now got a girlfriend called Margaret."*

- *"You don't waste any time do you, you lucky sod! I'd love to meet Billy again. Why don't I come over some time?"*

- *"Okay. Why don't the three of us go to the Abbey Cinema. They have a matinée on Saturday afternoon and there are a lot of girls that go."*

- *"That sounds great. Look I'll call for you about 3:30 then we'll cycle over to Bill's. Hey by the way, I'll ask John if he wants to come. He's pretty bored at the minute as well."*

The following afternoon John Lennon and Pete Shotton called at my place, 77 Lance Lane and we all went down to Bill's place. John Lennon had never met Billy Turner before although he had heard about him through Pete and myself. It was therefore going to be Billy Turner's first introduction to the"gang" although in actual fact he was automatically accepted in as "one of us" thanks to his sense of humour.

The Abbey Cinema matinée was really a place where boy would meet girl, boy would hold girl's hand, boy kisses girl, and whatever else besides. The four of us were regular visitors to the Abbey for the next few months, meeting a variety of girls. Many of their faces and names have long since been forgotten forty years down the line, but then we would generally forget their names after a week, so it's hardly surprising. It almost developed into a competition, vying to see who could meet the most different girls within a month. I don't know who won but I know we all eventually gained more experience in sexual matters as a result, as Pete Shotton relates in his book "John Lennon in My Life". Throughout these months towards the end of 1955, the nights being longer and the weather colder, I naturally spent more time at home, venturing out only once or twice a week, either to see Margaret Jones or to visit the local cinemas with John, Pete and sometimes Billy Turner.

One night at home I took a long look at myself in the mirror. My hair could do with a different look. I was always jealous of John and Pete's hair which was wavy whereas mine was absolutely straight and I had to constantly put vaseline on it to keep it in place.

- *"Mum can you do anything with my hair?"* I said in frustration. *"I need it to look more natural."*

- *"What you really need to do is to put a few curls in it then it will stay in place without all that Vaseline ."* said Mum. *"I'll do it for you if you like."*

At this suggestion of actually putting curls in my hair I started to back down. This was unheard of as far as I could tell; men having their hair permed. Eventually though I could see no other option than to have it done as she had suggested. I can remember it quite clearly : it was done a few days before I was due to meet Margaret Jones again, on our usual foursome date with Billy Turner and Beryl.

The resultant hairdo was quite pleasing, I thought as I looked in the mirror after it had been washed and dried. However, it was only permed at the front, the rest of my hair was straight as before! What 'stick' I was going to be in for at school the next day! The fear of what people might say began to creep in on me. Mum gave me a little lecture on what was normal and abnormal hair.

- *"I think it looks alright Len but all those people with naturally curly hair are probably desperate to have theirs straight. In fact straight hair is normal. it's just the fact that curly hair stays in place better that appeals to you, that's why you had it done isn't it? There was one other option, you could have had a crew cut like the Yankees."*

- *"No Mum, I think this is okay. I don't fancy having a crew cut. I wanted waves and I've got them. I'll just have to grin and bear all the comments I'll get from everyone."*

Funnily enough no one seemed that bothered at school the next day, apart from a few favourable remarks.

During this period of time leading up to Christmas and the New Year I spent my leisure time going out with Margaret; occasionally going to local dances, which I hated, or going to visit the cinema, usually with John Lennon and Pete Shotton. I can remember going to see "Rebel Without a Cause" with John and the gang but I was not really impressed by the film or by Dean's acting ability.

I think John felt the same way. John had been more impressed with the actor Marlon Brando in "On the Waterfront" which had been released in 1954. I think that this particular film with Brando, related more to the Liverpool "roots", with scenes of the New York waterfront and dockers squabbling over employment restrictions and union domination. Pete Shotton was more enthusiastic about Natalie Wood and what a "cracker" she was.

I usually looked forward to Christmas time but this particular year the celebrations were marred by my parents having to sort out family matters. This was because my grandfather Cartwright had died in December which meant that my grandmother had to move in with us, or she would have been on her own and she was suffering from Parkinson's disease. So Christmas was spent looking after Gran. Poor Gran because she had also begun to suffer from senile dementia and used to go on "walk abouts" in her nightie, I spent many an hour wandering the streets of Wavertree looking for her. It was finally agreed that my mother's eldest brother Walter would take Gran to his home in Bedford for a while.

At that moment I was looking forward to my fourteenth birthday, which was on the 6th of January, not for the presents or cards and the usual fuss, which I hated if it was directed at me, but because at 14 I felt that I would finally become a "real" teenager at last. I wouldn't have to lie to the girls I met about my age anymore.

At the Liverpool Institute towards the end of term prior to the Christmas holiday period there was a general relaxation in studies and students were invited on the last few days to bring in items for recreation purposes, such as games like chess or monopoly. I can recall that a certain Paul McCartney had brought in his guitar that Christmas and that together with his friend Ian James (who taught him many chords) they entertained some of their class mates. I was not involved in seeing the performance as I was not friendly with McCartney at the time, however Ivan Vaughan had started to make contact with Paul McCartney and they eventually became firm friends. This was because Ivan and Paul were now in the same language set at school.

Winter passed and Spring arrived to everyone's relief as it had seemed like a very long winter. Lonnie Donnegan's "Rock Island Line" entered the British pop charts in January 1956. Meanwhile the "gang", now with Billy Turner as a fully fledged member, were still looking for ways to create opportunities for fun and excitement. One incident remains quite clear in my mind, as it does in Pete Shotton's.

I met Ivan Vaughan one day walking along the dark corridors of the Institute between classes, I was just making my way to the playground for a quick cigarette.

- *"Hi there Ivy, how are things going?"*

- *"Oh, okay. It seems to be work, work, work. I am doing a lot of translating Greek to English at the moment."*
- *"That sounds just up your street Ivy, you know you love it really. I'm just on my way out for a smoke. Have you seen a lot of John and Pete lately?"*

- *"Not a lot but they'll probably start to venture out to Calderstones Park now that the weather is getting warmer. Are you still going out with that girl Margaret?"*

- *"Nah, I finished with her about a month ago. In fact I heard from Pete, who gives me a ring every now and again, that John left Barb (Barbara Baker) for a short while and went out with Margaret himself. It seems as though Lennon has set out to go out with every girl that I've been with."*

- *"Nah, you know what John's like, he treats women like dirt, yet they seem to come back for more."*

- *"Well if you see them tell them to meet me on the "bank" at the usual time, 2p.m. on Saturday and I'll get Billy Turner to come along. He desperately wants to see this place where we meet. Funny isn't it?"*

- *"Yeah, well okay I'll tell them. I'll have to go now. See you later Len."* With that we parted.

I met Billy Turner in the "smoker's den" and invited him to come to the "bank" the forthcoming Saturday. It was 2p.m. on an afternoon in late April 1956 and we were together again, re-united at the place that had begun to etch itself on our memories, Calderstones Park.

- *"I thought Bill was coming?"* Asked Pete as we all lay on the bank with our eyes turned upward to the blue sky.

- *"Don't worry, he'll be here. He has heard so much about this place that his curiosity won't let us down."*

Five minutes later Billy Turner appeared, arriving by the same path as I had a few moments earlier. He plonked himself down beside us.

- *"So this is the famous place that you've been telling me about. What's so special about a bit of sloping grass?"*

- "Bill, you wouldn't be saying that if you had been with us last summer. We had a great time."

Eventually Nigel Whalley joined us and we all felt as though it were a family re-union.

- "Hey Bill, we're off one day next week aren't we?"

- "Yeah, I think our teachers are having some kind of training day next Wednesday."

- "You lucky sods, having a day off. At Quarrybank our teachers never have training days," remarked Pete.

- "Having to teach, fellahs like you and Lennon I'd have thought they'd need special training," I joked.

We fell silent for a while as we drew heavily on our cigarettes. Then Lennon sat up suddenly.

- "Hey I've got a brilliant idea, why don't we (meaning himself and Pete

—Quarrybank High School.—

Shotton) *get Len and Bill to enroll as new boys at our school?"*

- *"Wednesday is the ideal day, we have Martin in the afternoons, we can tell him anything and he'll believe us."*

Billy Turner and I looked at one another to see if there was a hint of either one of us wanting to back away from the suggestion. It seemed to us a good way of "getting one over" on Quarrybank, who were our great rivals at cricket and football. On these occasions Quarrybank would usually emerge the victors. This was our chance to be victorious.

- *"Bill, I'm game if you are."*

Without hesitation Bill replied;

- *"Len, I'm already thinking what names we can give ourselves!"*

We spent the rest of the afternoon talking about the escapade, like an army platoon planning their next strike on enemy forces. We parted company at 4:30 p.m., Billy Turner and I returned together, having agreed to meet John and Pete during the lunch break outside Quarrybank School.

As we rode towards Lance Lane I said to Bill;

- *"Bill, I've been thinking, is it wise for you to get involved so soon after the break-in at the Institute's Armoury?"*

There had recently been some guns and blank ammunition stolen from the Cadet forces stores at the Institute and Billy had been targeted as a prime suspect.

- *"Oh don't worry Len. They didn't prove anything on that score. Anyway I was innocent,"* he looked at me with a cheeky grin, *"see you Monday."*

It was Sunday afternoon at Lance Lane after lunch.

- *"Mum did I tell you that we've got a day off on Wednesday? Our teacher's have a training day."*

- *"Oh have you? It's the first I've heard of it. I hope that you're telling the truth and not working up an excuse to skip school?"*

- *"Honestly Mum, it's the truth, you can ask Ivan if you like."*

- *"Okay, I believe you. Perhaps you can give me a hand on Wednesday in that case."*

- *"Okay Mum but it'll have to be in the morning because I have something planned for the afternoon. Ivan and I wanted to go swimming."*

- *"Swimming? You never go to the swimming baths, you can't even swim!"*

- *"Well Ivan is going to teach me a few strokes at Woolton swimming baths."*

- *"Good idea I'm glad that you have decided to do something more constructive with your friends than always playing the fool. Your school report this year was terrible. Every other comment was always, 'loves to play around too much'. "*

- *"Yeah I know Mum. I promise I'll try harder next year."*

Wednesday morning arrived and I helped my Mum out around the house, I had arranged to meet up with Billy at the Penny Lane roundabout on our bikes and then cycle up to Quarrybank, meeting up with John and Pete at 1:30 p.m. I had also arranged to take my school uniform with me to change into, as we had planned to tell Mr Martin that our parents had suddenly been transferred to Liverpool from abroad and that they had inadvertently bought the wrong uniforms. We never thought that they would link us up to the Institute that way.

We met John and Pete by the bike sheds, it was 1:25 p.m.

- *"Hey Len, what have you got in those bags?"* asked John.

- *"They're our school uniforms,"* I replied and proceeded to explain our little plan.

- *"I've got to hand it to you, you've got a nerve. I know Martin will believe you - you won't have a problem there, but if any other school master sees you they'll probably make enquiries at the Institute."*

- *"Well, we'll just have to sneak in and not let any of the other teachers see us."* said Billy objectively.

Billy and I made our way up to the Art Room, after having changed our clothes in the toilets and sat down at the vacant desks which were adjacent to the door just in case we needed to make a quick dash for it. John Lennon introduced us to Mr Martin. Pete Shotton wasn't there as he did not take this subject.

- *"Sir, we have two new boys that have only recently arrived in Liverpool."*

Mr Martin looked at us from where he was standing by his desk and there was a profound silence as he weighed up the situation.

- *"Why have you both suddenly appeared in my class? I know nothing about it. I'll have to see the head teacher about it afterwards. Meanwhile get yourselves some paper. I want you to draw the bowl of fruit which I am about to position in the middle of the room."*

John, Bill and I sat in separate desks which were all lined up together. Bill and myself then pulled out our Liverpool Institute scarves, which were green and black, out of our bags and wrapped them around our necks. I can remember that John Lennon's face when he saw us do this was a picture of incredulity as we started to draw. After a while Mr Martin walked up to see how we were getting on. He was more puzzled about why we were wearing hot woollen scarves on a reasonably warm day than about the fact that they were another school's colours.

- *"Are you two cold? It appears so or you wouldn't be wearing your scarves."*

- *"Yes sir, it's because we've been living abroad, in Australia, and we aren't used to this climate."*

- *"I see and what are your names?"* I remained the spokesman as Billy had his head down very near to the piece of paper, trying to stifle his laughter. *"My name is Garry."*

- *"Garry what?"*

- *"No Garry, that's my surname. Len is my christian name."*

- *"Oh I see, Leonard Garry."*

I never thought to give a false name. Billy was asked to give his name and gave his true name also. It was as though we had to provide an element of truth in order to make the whole escapade plausible. It was also more daring to give our real names and therefore more exciting. Martin wrote our names down on the class register. John Lennon meanwhile, was unusually quiet. I think he was in a state of shock and was even more amazed at the audacity of giving our real names. He was also surprised that Mr Martin was taking the whole charade so seriously.

—Quarrybank High School: The art room where Len and Billy Turner enrolled.—

Suddenly there was a knock at the door and a familiar head peered around - it was Pete Shotton who apparently couldn't resist making up an excuse to see how we were getting along.

- *"Yes Shotton, what do you want?"* asked Mr Martin, who knew Pete quite well.

- *"I've come to get my pen. I lent it to Lennon this morning Sir."*

- *"Is that correct Lennon? Have you got Shotton's pen? If so could you hand it over quickly, I don't like interruptions in my art class."*

As Pete Shotton would verify, John Lennon couldn't resist the chance to make the most fun out of the situation. Perhaps he felt a little out of the limelight, as he was normally at the hub of any mischief.

- *"What?"* He said, pretending he hadn't heard right and apparently engrossed in his drawing.

- *"Lennon, did you hear me? Have you got Shotton's pen?"*

John finally looked up and fixing Pete with a disdainful sneer said;

- *"I don't know what you are talking about Shotton. I haven't seen your pen; furthermore..."* by this time Billy and I were stifling our laughter with our scarves, *"...I strongly object to you coming in and disturbing me at work and I am sure that I'm also speaking on behalf of Mr Martin."*

It was quite a little speech, said with such sincerity, without a hint of a smile on his face that all poor Pete could do was apologize profusely to John and Mr Martin for disrupting the class. Mr Martin meanwhile turned his annoyance on Peter.

- *"I must say that I agree with Lennon on this occasion. Shotton, you will write 500 lines saying; 'I must not interrupt Mr Martin's Art Class', and let me have it first thing in the morning."*

John's face was still serious as Shotton left the room , enjoying his new role as the responsible, mature student. His self control and acting ability were truly remarkable.

The rest of the afternoon was spent in relative calm, with Billy and I trying our best to produce something reasonably artistic. Towards the end of the session we decided that we had had enough. We each in turn asked if we could be excused to go to the toilet. Billy disappeared first and I followed soon after in order that we might change into our everyday clothes.

Mr Martin never saw us again. Billy and I returned to school the next day acting as though nothing had happened, we didn't tell a soul except very close friends. Soon after there was a general enquiry and it eventually came to light that Quarrybank School had been the victim of a hoax played by two Liverpool Institute lads.

A week passed by and we didn't hear anything and therefore assumed that the incident had blown over. However, one morning in assembly, the headmaster J.R.Edwards made a remark referring to the incident that had recently taken place whereby our old rivals Quarrybank had been "infiltrated by the enemy". Following this announcement, during which he had never mentioned our names, we received knowing smiles from the teachers, who must have been told that it had been Billy and myself. I was amazed that they took it so well, we received a sharp reprimand and a warning from the headmaster not to do it again but that was all.We were the heroes of the school that week.

Throughout the coming months my school work went from bad to worse. I was still not taking school seriously, the only thing I enjoyed was being able to get the class in an uproar, reacting to my funny remarks.

A similar state of affairs was happening to John Lennon and Pete Shotton at Quarrybank; they were constantly getting into trouble by "acting the clown" in class. We had our usual school photograph taken in late April 1956 in which I still had my curly hair at the front. I mention this fact because it helps me to pinpoint the dates when different things happened later on in the year that were critical to the story.

It was soon after the school photograph that I decided to change my hairstyle as it was becoming a constant source of bother trying to keep it in place. I opted for a semi-crew cut.

All through that summer of 1956, the gang were in residence again on the bank at Calderstones Park but with the addition of Billy Turner, who was now a regular visitor to our afternoon "sessions". Although we had heard Lonnie Donnegan's skiffle recordings they did not captivate our imagination. John Lennon wasn't "hooked" until he heard Elvis Presley's recording of "Heartbreak Hotel". This was the seed that had been cast abroad and Lennon's musical ear and heart were ready to receive it. The love of it grew inside of him from that moment. All through the autumn days and nights of 1956 it germinated, it was growing secretly, undetectable visually but inevitably it sprang forth as the first thoughts of forming his own band.

The Formation Of The Quarrymen

There has been a great deal of speculation amongst Beatle historians and fans as to what the exact date was when the Quarrymen formed. In trying to pinpoint this date following interviews with the original members Eric Griffiths, Pete Shotton and Rod Davis I realised that it was virtually impossible to determine, as the people who were there (the only people with genuine recollections worth listening to) could not agree on a specific time and date. My personal opinion and recollection was that it was at the end of 1956, because I know that I joined at the age of fourteen and I was not fifteen until January 1957. Rod Davis and Eric Griffiths are of the opinion that it was late 1956. Mark Lewisohn's book 'The Beatles Chronicles' puts the date as March 1957, but this may have been the date when we first played in public.

The Events Leading Up To The Formation Of The Group

In 1953, when he was thirteen years old, John Lennon had renewed acquaintance with his estranged mother Julia who he discovered did not live very far away from Mendips in Menlove Aveneue, where he was living at the time. He started paying her regular visits, enjoying her company and found they had a mutual love of music. She had an old banjo and was constantly playing and singing when she wasn't listening to gramophone records. She eventually taught John a few banjo chords and it sparked off an interest within John to learn to play the guitar, particularly now that the likes of Elvis Presley and Lonnie Donnegan had burst onto the popular music scene with such impetus.

At Quarrybank High School in early September 1956 a lad called George Lee, who was friendly with Eric Griffiths and John Lennon, perceived that John's interest in the guitar was increasing and so (according to Eric) suggested to John that he form his own group. In a recent interview Eric stated, "George was a cocky type of character who was very good at coming up with ideas but had no idea how to put the ideas into effect." Never the less the seed was sown in John Lennon's mind.

John promptly looked for someone to discuss the idea with and so he turned to his best friend Pete Shotton. One day in late September 1956 John and Pete were walking across the school grounds when John suddenly blurted out what had been on his mind for over a week.

"Pete, I've been thinking for a while now of forming my own group - you know, a skiffle group."

Pete was silent for a few moments.

"Well I hope you don't think I'm going to join your little band." Pete said quite sharply.

"Ah eh Pete. Lonnie Donnegan formed his own group and look where he got to - the top of the hit parade. I've got my own guitar now."

John had cajoled and pestered Mimi and Julia for his own guitar and eventually Julia agreed to buy him a second hand instrument at Hessy's music shop in Liverpool.

Pete was still not impressed.

John continued, *"All we need to start with is a washboard and an old tea chest."*

"I don't know John I'll have to think about it."

"What's there to think about? You can play the washboard, you don't have to have any musical ability to play that. Come on Pete."

John could see a spark of interest on Pete's face now.

"It'll be a laugh - even if it doesn't come to anything. Let's give it a try."

Upon seeing his friend's eagerness and enthusiasm, not wanting to let him down and knowing that John would not give up pestering him, Pete Shotton agreed to give it a go.

Then There Were Two

Pete then found an old washboard in his back garden shed and his mother provided him with an old tea chest which had been lying around in her wool shop in Quarry Street. John and Pete then constructed the tea chest bass using an old broom handle and a piece of string. John and Pete had three instruments in their group but only two players so they enquired at Quarrybank whether anyone would like to have a go on the tea chest bass. The only taker for this casual invitation was a chap called Bill Smith.

Then There Were Three

The budding young pop stars looked for a place to try out their little group and found it in the form of a disused air raid shelter in the back garden of Pete Shotton's home at No: 83 Vale Road. They played skiffle numbers such as 'Cumberland Gap' and 'Rock Island Line'. These first rehearsals of the band with no name began in late September 1956.
John and Pete looked around for more members. I must mention that soon after John obtained his guitar, before any thought of forming a group had crossed his mind, he linked up with the only person in Quarrybank who he knew had a guitar and that was Eric Griffiths. These two were keen to learn how to play. One day they came across an advertisement in a local newspaper stating that guitar tuition was available in the Hunt's Cross area of South Liverpool, which was not far away from Woolton Village. John and Eric went along but according to Eric, *"We both found the lessons to be too boring. We were looking for a quick way to play tunes on our guitars - there was too much theory - we packed it in after the first couple of lessons."*
John and Pete then asked Eric Griffiths to join their group.

Then There Were Four — John Lennon, Pete Shotton, Bill Smith, Eric Griffiths

It was not long after that when another Quarrybank student named Rod Davis was asked to join as they knew Rod owned and played a banjo. They weren't particularly bothered what instruments their new recruits could play - just that they could play the numbers.

Then There Were Five

While these new members joined the group they would occasionally practice at Julia's house or in the air raid shelter. Julia's house was preferred however because they were allowed to practice on occasion in the bathroom in order to obtain more echo on their instruments and vocals.

One Saturday afternoon in October 1956 the group of fledgling musicians gathered at Eric Griffiths house for a practice session. Eric was friendly with a lad called Colin Hanton who he knew had a set of drums. Eric was persuaded by the other members of the group to pop around to Colin's house, as he did not live very far away, they asked Colin if he would like to bring his drums around. Colin agreed and so...

Then There Were Six

They then discussed various names for the new group and eventually arrived at the name 'Blackjacks' which was discarded after one week as nobody could relate the name to anybody or anything. It was not long before the name 'Quarrymen' was suggested - the main influence being from a phrase taken from Quarrybank High's school song.

"Quarrymen strong before our birth."

Furthermore, Woolton itself was renowned for it's sandstone quarry which was providing building stone to the Anglican Cathedral under construction at the time.

By late October 1956 it was decided that Bill Smith's services were no longer required because he never turned up for any practice sessions. During this period Ivan Vaughan or Nigel Whalley would stand in as tea chest bass players. It was during the last few days of the half term holiday taken in the last week of October 1956 that I was asked to join the group as the tea chest bass player. I had heard Ivan Vaughan talk about the group to me at school but I had no intention of asking if I could join until Ivan told me that the invitation had been made by John and Pete. I was glad to accept, although for me it was only a means whereby I could have the opportunity to sing alongside the likes of John Lennon. I didn't particularly look forward to playing the tea chest bass. And so the Quarrymen skiffle group was formed.

Pete Shotton, John Lennon and The Tea Chest Bass

Thursday 11th November 1956: Time - 3:30 p.m.

John Lennon and Pete Shotton, the two members of the newly formed Quarrymen Skiffle Group collected their respective bicycles from the shed at Quarrybank school. It was a relatively warm afternoon for mid November and so they took their time.

- *"Listen John, why did you let Bill Smith join the group? He never turns up to any of the rehearsals and I can't stand the guy anyway."*

- *"Well Pete, he was keen enough to join in the first place but perhaps we should be looking to replace him because he's so unreliable."*

- *"What about Len Garry, you know he can sing and he has a good sense of humour."*

- *"Yeah Len sounds like just the man."*

By this time Pete and John had reached the Harthill Road entrance to Calderstones Park, (the entrance that has statues depicting the four seasons). Pete and John quite often rode through the park on their way to school if they were short of time as it cut quite a few corners and about 10 minutes off their journey. However, they were in no rush now so they dismounted and ambled along, intent on letting the soothing surroundings of the park clear their minds from the day.

John's interest in the group had grown immensely since the first rehearsal had taken place in Pete's back garden shed: he had lost all interest in school and academic work by this time. Pete Shotton was glad to lose Bill Smith from the group as he had never got on with him, in fact he had been Pete's enemy at school, he was only in the group because he had been the only one keen enough to offer to play the tea chest bass.

By this time the two boys pushing their bicycles had reached the old mansion house that was used as a café in those days, it was a rather imposing building that fitted in beautifully with the surrounding parkland.

- *"Fancy a drink?"* asked Pete.

- *"I don't think it's open,"* said John, *"don't forget it's not summer."*

Pete went to see if there was any life in the place and came to the conclusion that John was right -everything was shut up for the winter. They sauntered on past the Mansion house and through the narrow path that led through the large rhododendron bushes. In the summer months these bushes held great delight for children who called them "monkey trees" as they were so easy to climb. John and Paul recalled such activities as they strode past.

- *"It's difficult to imagine the summer again,"* said Pete as the park was almost deserted, even though it was such a nice evening.

- *"It makes a change though,"* said John, who was appreciating the park's quiet winter beauty as the winter sun started to set beyond the park lake.

They pushed on with their bikes down the grassy slope that led to our "second home" in the summer time - the "bank", where we had spent most of our summer holidays.

- *"We need to fix a new rehearsal date,"* said John. *"Particularly now that we're getting Len as the tea chest bass player."*

- *"Okay, you say where and when."*

- *"First of all we have to tell Bill Smith that he is no longer wanted and ask Len if he wants to join."*

- *"I'm pretty sure he'll accept,"* said Pete. *"You know how much he loves to sing but we'll leave the practice session until we've sorted the group out."*

By this time they had reached the side of the boating lake. The rowing boats were all locked up for the winter season and the only activity were the ducks flying in and landing on the lake like airplanes gliding onto a runway.

- *"We don't see much of Len these days,"* remarked John, *"does he hibernate in the winter or what?"*

- *"Well he knocks about with Billy Turner. They live quite close to each other so Len tends to knock around with Bill in the winter months. Well, you pass a message to Ivy* (Ivan Vaughan) *asking Len if he wants to join."*

- *"Okay, I'll mention it to Ivan."* Said John

It was reaching 5:00 and starting to get dark now, the two pals had reached the small exit by the tennis courts. They mounted their bikes, turned right into

Menlove Avenue and from there it was only a five minute dash to Mendips.

Just before they parted at the corner of Vale Road Pete asked John: *"By the way where did we leave the tea chest, did we leave it at Ivan's or Nigel's?"* (These were the only two places where it was usually kept).

- *"I'm pretty sure it's at Nigel's."* said John and with that the two friends parted company.

John, as usual, did not change down a gear as he approached the gates of Mendips - no such chance! He bumped up on the pavement (as we all had a habit of doing with our bikes), in other words; he lifted the front wheels by pulling on the drop handlebars of his Raleigh Lenton so that it would clear the curb at approximately 15 m.p.h. and whiz into the small driveway, just missing one of the many cats his Aunt Mimi would lovingly care for. He stepped off his bike as though he were a cowboy from a wild west rodeo and parked the bicycle by the side of the garage. John always went in the side entrance that led into Aunt Mimi's living room, at the back of the semi-detached house - he never used the front entrance (except when he was leaving).

- *"Is that you John?"* called Mimi from the kitchen.

- *"No it's the milkman."* came John's cutting reply

- *"Don't be funny I'm not in the mood for your silly jokes John. I want a word with you."*

- *"What have I done now?"*

- *"It's not what you've done it's what you haven't done."* replied Mimi as John threw his jacket on the living room chair. *"Ever since you've started this stupid group your school work has gone steadily down hill and it's important that you get the grades in the GCE certificates if you want to get a decent career. You're never in and I never see you doing any homework these days."*

John pretended he hadn't heard a word; although he thought the world of his Aunt and was, deep down, very grateful for all the sacrifices she was making in caring for him, the mere thought of doing any homework filled him with horror.

- *"Okay, okay, don't go on and don't worry about me I'll succeed, just you wait and see. Anyway, what's for tea?"* He smiled his disarming smile and with that any further discussion about his academic future dissolved immediately.

John was 16 years of age and had adopted the appearance of a middle class Teddy Boy: wearing tight drainpipe trousers and sporting a thick, wavy D.A. (ducks arse) at the back of his head. His whole interest now revolved around music and all he looked forward to was getting the lads together again for the next rehearsal.

- *"Tea? Oh, I've got you some fish and chips in the oven,"* said Mimi, *"I've had mine. I didn't know you would be back so late."*

- *"Well I came home with Pete and we walked through 'Colly'park,"* (an affectionate name for Calderstones).

John gave himself a quick wash in the kitchen and then ran up to his bedroom, he didn't like Mimi to see his schoolbooks because they were full of cartoon characters and comic verses, not full of English essays etc. as they should have been. He grabbed his guitar which he kept under his bed and tried out the chords to Gene Vincent's "Be Bopa Lula". It sounded better in the bathroom, he thought, it acted like an echo chamber as there were very hard surfaces which made the sound bounce back to him as he played. He quickly rushed into the bathroom with his guitar, turned on the tap as though he was getting washed and played; "Be Bopa Lula - she's my baby - Be Bopa Lula - I don't mean maybe."

- *"John...John! John!"* Eventually John heard Mimi's voice through the bathroom door.*"I'm not keeping the oven on any longer, hurry up and get your tea."*

It was now approaching 6 o'clock and John was starving hungry yet it still seemed like a big decision -to carry on practising or eat. His stomach was the winner this time.

John was thinking of where the band could have their next rehearsal as he wolfed down his tea. Maybe Julia (his mother) could accommodate them this coming Saturday? He knew Eric Griffiths' Mum had the day off and so Eric's house was out of the question (this was the normal venue for Saturday practices). First, he needed to contact his friend Ivan Vaughan to get him to ask me if I wanted to join the group and secondly, he needed to go round to his mothers (Julia's) to see if the group could rehearse there on Saturday. It was now Thursday night.

- *"Mimi, I've got something to see to tonight. I've got to go round to Julia's and Ivy's to arrange something."*

- *"What?"* came Mimi's voice from the kitchen; she couldn't hear very well above the noise of the twin tub washing machine.

John rose up from his meal and went towards the kitchen, *"I've got some things to sort out tonight,"* he shouted, *"can't you turn that thing off, I can't hear myself speak?"*

Mimi came out of the kitchen to where John was standing plate in hand, still finishing off his fish and chips, John stooped down on one knee, plate in hand.

- *"Dear Aunt Mimi please accept this small gift for everything,"* (it was a dirty plate with a few half eaten chips and remnants of brown sauce and vinegar). *"Look, what I've been trying to say for the last ten minutes is that I've got to go out to arrange a few things. Is that okay?"*

- *"Don't act stupid John,"* she smiled, (she was used to his antics by now). *"Okay but don't be too late will you?"*

It was about 7 p.m. by this time and so he went up to his room to give his hair a final comb and quickly made his bed. He decided that he wouldn't take his bicycle as it was not far to walk to Ivan Vaughan's in Vale Road and in order to visit his mother he could cut across Allerton golf links.

He knocked on Ivan's door. Eventually Ivan's sister, Bernice came to the door.

- *"Is Ivy in?"*

- *"Yes but he's busy doing his homework."*

- *"I only want to see him for a minute, just to pass a message on."*

Bernice shouted for her brother to come to the front door. Ivan Vaughan was always doing his homework (Greek to English translation) and hated any interruptions. However it was quite rare that John called for him personally so he thought it must be important.

- *"What's up John?"*

- *"Look Ivy, I want you to ask Len if he'll take over the tea chest bass from Bill Smith."*

- *"Why?"*

- *"Because Bill never turns up to rehearsals and we agreed - that is Shotton and I - to have Len in the group."*

- *"How do you know he wants to be in it?"* asked Ivan.

Ivan felt a little hurt that John had not asked him to join the group as he himself would sometimes have a go on the tea chest, as it was usually kept in his back garden shed.

- *"Just ask him, I know he'll accept, he loves music and he's in our gang now anyway."*

Ivan and I had been very close school mates from when we were about 11 years old but now, three years later, we had parted company at school. Ivan had moved up into the 'A' stream whilst I had moved into the 'D' stream. However we were still good friends simply because I had become close friends with John Lennon, Pete Shotton and the other members of the Quarrymen.

- *"Okay, I'll ask him. By the way John, where is the tea chest because it isn't in my shed. Check with Nigel next door."* (Nigel Whalley, the Quarrymen's manager lived immediately next door).

- *"Okay I will, thanks Ivy."*

John was aware that Ivan was a little peeved that he was about to ask me to come into the group and tried to re-assure him in the best way he knew that Ivy was still part of the "gang" and that he didn't want to lose his friendship. John was finding even at this early stage in his musical career that forming a band was similar to running a business, as the assumed leader he would have to make decisions that would sometimes offend those close to him. He was finding it hard. Nevertheless, John knew that Ivan's school work was more important to him than taking a main part in the group.

- *"Ivy, I need people who are going to take it seriously and turn up to practice sessions. I know that most of your time is taken up with Greek and Latin. If by any chance Len doesn't turn up you know you can take your turn."*

It was rather a patronising reply and anybody else might have been offended at this conciliatory offer but not Ivan.

- *"Yeah if I'm free I'd be glad to. Now I'll have to go. I'll see you tomorrow and let you know what he says."*

John was satisfied at that and felt quite pleased with himself at his handling of the situation. Little did he know there was to be another mini-crisis around the corner that would necessitate rather drastic action on his part.

John didn't feel like knocking on Nigel Whalley's door, he felt certain that Nigel would have the chest secure in his shed at the back of the garage. He did not want to face Nigel Whalley's father either and he usually answered the door whenever John called. He was a frightening figure of a man; about 6'2" high and an inspector in the police force. John knew that Nigel's father did not like him, in fact he knew that Nigel used to get beaten if he misbehaved. No, he certainly didn't fancy facing him tonight.

It was getting near 8 o'clock and it had turned quite cold now. John needed someone to talk to but decided he couldn't go to his mothers (Julia's) after all as he didn't fancy walking all that way across the golf links on a cold November evening. Anyway, there was no desperate reason to see her to ask permission to practice, he could always ride over there on Saturday morning - yeah, that's what he would do. He turned right out of Ivan's house, along Vale Road towards Pete Shotton's house.

Pete Shotton's home was situated about 100 yards from Ivan's and was a slightly smaller, detached house. Pete's bedroom was the small one over the front porch and as John approached he could see a light on in his bedroom. Instead of knocking on the front door in the usual way John decided to throw some soil

—Pete Shotton's house in Vale Road - Len would whistle passing by on his bike.—

from the front garden at the window in order to attract Pete's attention. He didn't feel like talking to Mr and Mrs Shotton at this moment in time so he tried Pete directly.

- *"Pete, hsst, Pete."*

After a few minutes the window opened and a shock of blond curly hair appeared.

- *"What the B. hell do you want. I can't come out tonight. I've been confined to barracks."*

- *"Awe Pete I feel a bit pissed off. Can't you sneak out, we could go to the Milk Bar for a drink or get a couple of bottles from the Off Licence."*

Pete shook his head out of the window.

- *"John I'd love to but it's more than my life's worth right now."*

The fact was that prior to the celebration of November 5th (on which England celebrates the burning of Guy Fawkes, who tried to blow up parliament), John Lennon and I had set fire to the bonfire on a piece of waste ground called "the tip" which was almost directly opposite Pete's house. Rumours had spread that

—'The Tip' in 1997 where Lennon and the gang set bonfire.—

John Lennon and Pete Shotton were responsible for the misdemeanour although Pete had nothing to do with it. By all accounts Pete's parents had got wind of the rumour and consequently had confined Pete to the house for a week.

- *"Alright, I'll see you tomorrow. Meet me at the usual place on the corner of Vale Road. I think I'll call in on Barbara."*

"Barbara" was Barbara Baker, John's steady girlfriend, (who used to be mine) who lived quite near in Linkstor Road, off Quarry Street not very far away. Barbara had been John's girlfriend now for over a year and John also regarded her as someone he could confide in as a friend. He was finding it difficult as there seemed to be so much going on in his life at that time. He experienced profound dissatisfaction at school, finding the teachers (apart from the arts teacher) too concerned with him getting his certificate. He was not interested in sport, mainly because he could not see very well and felt self conscious about wearing glasses. His Aunt Mimi was also at him all the time, trying to get him to conform and study and he didn't really like the thought of letting her down. Yet when he went over to see Julia (his mother) there was a completely different attitude from her. She didn't seem concerned about his progress at school, just as long as he was happy and she would always encourage him on his guitar and take an interest in the progress of the Quarrymen. John was just thinking that it would be nice to talk to Barbara as he turned the corner of the road that led up to Quarry Street. He heard footsteps behind him and someone calling his name.

- *"John, John!"* It was Nigel Whalley running after him. *"John,"* he gasped, trying to catch his breath. *"John, I don't know where the tea chest is. It isn't in my back shed. I think Bill Smith must have taken it back to his place."*

- *"What! What did you let him take it for? You know we always keep it at yours or Ivy's. I've got to break the news to Bill tomorrow that he's no longer in the group and if I do that do you think he's going to give us the tea chest back? Not likely. Awe shit. Okay Nige. I was going to see Barbara but now I think I'll just head back home, come on, we'll walk back together."*

With that the two of them walked back along Vale Road towards Nige's house. Another problem to sort out thought John.

- *"Nige I was going to call at your place just to check if you had the tea chest but I didn't feel like facing your Dad."* (Particularly after the bonfire episode).

- *"Well I've just seen Ivan and he told me that you called. What are you going to do?"*

- *"We'll have to steal it back. It's as simple as that. Shotton and I made that chest. He's got a bloody cheek! He lives up in Childwall doesn't he?"*

- *"Yeah I think so. When will you do it?"*

- *"Tomorrow after I break the news to him that he's no longer in the group. Shotton and I will sag* (play truant) *off school."* (Tomorrow being Friday). *"No one will notice as we have the Art session on Fridays."*

John parted company at Nigel's house and arrived back at Mimi's at about 9 p.m. He suddenly felt tired as he let himself in the back door. Mimi was in the lounge with the radio on listening to a play.

- *"Is that you John?"*

- *"Yeah. Look I'll feed the cats then I think I'll go to bed."*

- *"Alright love. See you in the morning, goodnight."*

John performed his small chore and then returned to his bedroom thinking what a waste of an evening it had been. It didn't seem to have achieved anything, only

— 'Mendips' - Aunt Mimi's house in Menlove Avenue: John Lennon's home.—

leaving him with another problem to resolve. Ah well, I'll think about that tomorrow, he thought. With that he had a quick wash, read a few lines from Edgar Allen Poe's mysteries and then fell fast asleep in no time.

Despite having gone to sleep exhausted John had a rather restless night. He was awakened in the early hours of the morning by the sound of cats fighting just beneath his bedroom window. It was quite a regular occurrence and usually involved one or two of Aunt Mimi's beloved cat collection. John opened the casement window of the small bay and at the same time looked for something to throw at the cats. Just as he found something suitable however, the cats decided to go elsewhere. He got back into bed but could not get back to sleep as his mind started to dwell on events happening in his life.

The main theme of his thoughts were on the newly formed band of youngsters he now called the Quarrymen. He was excited that he had found a new outlet for another of his God-given talents and was enjoying every opportunity given to him to demonstrate it. He would love to play the guitar in a more professional way and determined in his heart to practice on it as much as he could. He had not the slightest thought that it might lead to a full time career in music but now it was in his blood and needed expression. His mind wandered slightly as he heard a sound coming from the landing outside his bedroom door. He usually left the door slightly ajar as Sally the dog often made a scratching protest to come in and sleep on his bed. The sound was Mimi going through to the bathroom.

He needed some source of comfort and so he reached into the small locker that was beside his bed. He had about two Senior Service cigarettes from the packet of five he had bought earlier that evening (Senior Service was his favourite brand). He propped himself up on his pillows and using the cigarette packet as an ashtray picked up one of his favourite books that he never tired of. It was one of Richard Crompton's "Just William" series about a youngster that was always getting into mischief. He read a couple of pages but his mind was wandering again.

He looked at the small alarm clock - it was just 2 a.m. He usually set the alarm for 7:30 but this time he decided to alter it to 8 a.m. that would give him a bit longer in bed because at this rate he would not get much sleep. He threw the book down in frustration and his eyes strayed across the bedroom to the large poster of Elvis Presley fixed with drawing pins to his bedroom door. How he would love to be Elvis, he thought. He had read the story of how Elvis had started his career by going into a small recording studio to make a record for his mother's birthday. Why, he wondered, aren't there any places in Liverpool like that where he could go and do a similar thing? He wouldn't have to bother getting the group together then. But what would he sing? The only songs he really liked were the ones such as "Be Bopa Lula" or an occasional Buddy Holly song. Perhaps he could use his writing talent as well as his musical one and make up his own songs? It was another thought that he put on his list of things to pursue in the future.

He finished his cigarette, switched off the bedroom light, for which he had to get out of bed as he didn't have the luxury of a bedroom lamp, then dropped back into bed. Sally was disturbed for a moment and then decided to curl up on the bottom of his bed. He was grateful as the warmth of the little dog's body helped to keep his feet warm.

His alarm went off as planned at 8:00 a.m. prompt. John Lennon was awake instantly but turned over in his bed, he had plenty of time. Then it was suddenly five minutes past. Shit! He thought it's late. He usually met his best friend Pete Shotton on the corner of Vale Road by 8:00 a.m. Pete would be waiting. He took a quick glance out of his small bay window, looking right towards the Vale Road end, he could see Pete waiting at the corner leaning on his bicycle. He got dressed in double quick time, collected his small exercise book in which he had portrayed his "Daily Howl" series of cartoons, collected his Raleigh Lenton from the garage and without uttering a word to Mimi who had been in the kitchen preparing his breakfast, hopped onto his bicycle to meet Pete.

- *"Pete what time is it?"*

- *"It's 8:15 a.m. what happened to you? I'm the one whose usually late."* Said Pete.

- *"Oh I've just had a sleepless night. The cats woke me up and things have been churning over in my mind all night."*

The school was about 15 minutes away from where they lived.

- *"John, Nige says the tea chest's missing."*

- *"Well we haven't lost it. This means that someone's nicked it* (stolen it). *I bet it's Bill Smith."*

- *"Why would it be Bill? We haven't told him he's no longer in the group yet."*

- *"I know we haven't told him officially but I think he's got wise to the fact and taken it back to his place."*

- *"Well if that's the case, we'll just have to nick it back. The cheek of the guy. We made that tea chest with our own tender hands: it's a craftsman's work of art."* said Pete with a sardonic grin.

- *"Look Pete, we'll have to sag off school this afternoon,"* said John as they approached Quarry Bank School.

"What lesson have we got this afternoon?" asked Pete.

- *"Art with Martini."* (This was a nickname for Mr Martin the art teacher).

- *"That's okay. We'll put out our cardboard cut outs and fix them to the desk. He won't know the difference,"* joked Pete and they both burst out laughing.

The morning at school passed quite quickly, the two pals had arranged to see Bill Smith during morning break time. Prior to meeting Bill, John and Pete agreed the following plan:

- *"Pete don't start accusing Bill of taking the chest bass. Let's ask him if we can arrange a practice for the group at his house on Saturday (the next day), say in the afternoon. He'll be chuffed at that. If he says okay we'll then ask him where he lives. That way he'll not get suspicious and we'll also find out where he lives."*

- *"Good thinking my son,"* said Pete and that was that.

That morning at Quarrybank school:

The lads were in a corner of the playground just behind the bicycle sheds where they gathered together to have a quick fag (smokers corner). It was about 10:45 a.m. John and Pete had just lit up when Bill Smith sauntered over.

- *"Hi there Bill"* said Pete trying to act friendly, *"have a fag"*. Pete offered Bill one of his "Passing Clouds" (oval shaped cigarettes).

- *"Aw thanks Pete. I've never had one of these oval shaped fags before."*

- *"Look Bill, Pete and I were thinking of having a group practice tomorrow. Could we have it at your place, say, Saturday afternoon?"*

- "Yeah that would be okay because my Mum and Dad will be out so we'll have the place to ourselves."

- *"That's great,"* said John, *"whereabouts do you live?"*

Bill gave John his address which was in Childwall in the South area of Liverpool.

- *"By the way Bill, do you know where the tea chest has got to?"*

- *"Yeah, don't you remember? I took it home with me after that session at your Mum's place."*

- *"Oh yeah, I remember,"* said John condescendingly, *"let's make it for about 2 o'clock."*

- *"Okay that's agreed."* With that the lads parted company and went back to their lessons.

- *"The flipping cheek. I don't remember him taking it back after that practice and we didn't give him permission anyway even if he did."* said John. *"Lets give him the boot. I know, we'll wait till lunchtime and then tell him."*

It was a devious plan but Pete and John agreed to it.

- *"We'll have to inform Rod Davies and Eric Griffiths before we do though because we're all in this together."*

- *"Yeah I know but don't tell Rod and Eric about our plan to get the tea chest back, you know what they're like,"* said John.

Lunchtime came at 12 noon. Rod Davies and Eric Griffiths were walking across the school playing fields to go to the school canteen for lunch. They were both quite respectable looking boys Rod Davies looking quite studious in his rather large spectacles and Eric looking as smart as ever in his neatly pressed black trousers, white shirt and his Quarry Bank school tie that was always neatly fastened with a tie pin.

John Lennon and Pete Shotton spotted them from their usual spot behind the bike sheds and called them over.

- *"Listen lads, we're going to tell Bill Smith he's no longer needed. Is that okay?"* asked John.

Eric and Rod were not surprised at the decision and agreed. It was nearing 12:30

by this time and the first dinner session was under way at school.

- *"I think Bill is on second dinners,"* said John, *"so he should still be around."* Second dinners meant the second lunch session as it took place in two shifts.

John and Pete eventually spotted Bill and told him he was no longer required.

- *"That's a dirty thing to do, just an hour ago you wanted to practice at my place. What's brought this about?"* Bill was obviously quite distressed when John broke the news.

- *"Well we want people to be committed to the group and turn up for practices and to be honest we don't like you very much either."* answered John who was sick of the situation by this time and had decided to get straight to the point.

- *"Yeah,"* agreed Pete, *"you know we don't get on and never will do, so you're out. Okay? End of story!"*

- *"Well you needn't think you'll get the tea chest back."* shouted Bill as he stormed off angrily.

- *"Phew!"* said John. *"What a relief that's over with. I hate falling out with people. Listen, we'll have to forge a note to give to Martin to get time off this afternoon because we've sagged off so many times that we'll be up before the headmaster if we don't."*

Pete agreed and obtained some writing paper from the general office, together with an envelope and wrote the following in his best handwriting;

Dear Sir,
Following the sudden bereavement of his Aunt Gertrude could you kindly excuse Pete Shotton from attending classes this day. Furthermore, as John Lennon is closely related he will be absent also,
yours sincerely,
Mrs Shotton.

John looked at the letter and giggled to himself.

- *"Who the hell is Aunt Gertrude? They're bound to smell a rat at that one Shotto!"*

- *"I know, we'll leave the letter on Martini's desk before the afternoon session starts."*

The letter was duly left on the desk and the two friends hopped onto their bikes and cycled towards Menlove Avenue. As they were approaching Mendips John realised they really needed to go back to his mother's house (Julia's) in Springwood, as Mimi and Pete's Mum would immediately send them back to school with a sharp reprimand. Not so Julia, she was only too happy to see the boys and immediately prepared them something to eat; eggs, bacon and fried bread washed down with a giant mug of coffee. They gulped down the food as they were both ravenously hungry.

- *"Look Mum,"* said John,*"Pete and I have something to do this afternoon and as much as we'd like to stay and keep you company this thing needs our urgent action."* John told his mother that Pete and he were planning to steal back the tea chest from Bill Smith's in Childwall. *"How do we get to Childwall? I think it's in a street near Childwall fiveways."* This was an area where five roads converged into a roundabout - hence "Fiveways".

- *"We'll have to get two buses at least. Get the 72 or number 4 along Menlove and get the 61 bus at the top of Green Lane. That'll get us to Fiveways."* answered Pete, who knew the bus routes quite well.

It was about 2:30 that Friday afternoon and John Lennon and Pete Shotton walked together to the bus stop on Menlove Avenue, just opposite Vale Road. They didn't have to wait long for a 72 bus which would take them about three stops along Menlove Avenue. As they boarded the bus they were just making their way along the gangway of the lower deck when John suddenly spotted someone he knew.

- *"Psst Pete, there's my Uncle, Cissie Smith, Mimi's brother."*

Cissie (as he was nicknamed), was an English teacher at the Liverpool Institute and for some unknown reason was travelling on the lower deck.

- *"Come on quick. Upstairs."*

The two lads scarpered upstairs, breathing a sigh of relief that he didn't see them. They lit up a fag each to steady their nerves, (smoking on the upper deck was allowed in those days).

They got off the bus at Green Lane, not very far from the main entrance to

Calderstones park and waited for a number 61 bus.

- *"Flipping heck!"* Said Pete, *"I don't need this, that was a close call. Why do we always seem to be living on a knife edge all the time? Trouble seems to stick to us like a leech."*

- *"Relax,"* said John, *"he didn't see us."*

It seemed as though they waited for ages for a number 61 and the time was just after 3 p.m. They finally arrived at Childwall fiveways and made their way to Bill Smith's house, John having written the address down on a scrap of paper.

- *"Hey, wait a minute,"* said Pete, *"how do we know there won't be someone in the house, or whether Bill hasn't got a great big dog waiting to sink it's teeth into us?"*

- *"I know for a fact that he hasn't got a dog and his Mum and Dad will be out at work. Don't worry, you don't half fret. Relax, you're starting to give me the jitters. Oh here we are..."*

They finally arrived at the quiet, tree lined road and John looked at the scrap of paper for the house number on the directions. *"There it is,"* said John looking at a quiet, deserted, reasonably maintained semi-detached house that was set back from the main road.

- *"Don't be daft!"* Said Pete. *"Get your glasses on, you've got the wrong one."*

John always felt self conscious about wearing his glasses and had therefore squinted hard trying to decipher his writing without putting his glasses on.

- *"There it is,"* said Pete. *"Hey there's a car in the driveway, we'd better go very carefully."*

- *"I know, we'll test out whether anyone's in."* Said John.

- *"How are you going to do that?"* asked Pete. *"We haven't got our Gasman's uniforms on, we can hardly pretend we're going to read the gas meter."*

- *"What we'll do is that I'll knock on the door and ask if they have seen my lost cat called Ginger, just in case someone's in. His Mum and Dad don't know me anyway."*

With that John rang the door bell. Pete in the meantime hid behind the front garden wall. John rang the door bell for at least five minutes but there was no reply.

- *"Psst Pete. It's okay, there's no one in,"* called John, who appeared to be talking into thin air, as Pete Shotton was nowhere to be seen. Eventually Pete arose from his hiding place and joined up with John.

- *"How the hell are we going to get in?"* Asked Pete.

- *"Go around the side and see if there's a window open."*

In those days there were no such things as security alarms and many housewives would even leave their windows slightly open, especially in a respectable area. There was not much danger as burglary was extremely rare. Sure enough Pete found that the kitchen window had been left slightly open, about an inch. There was just enough room to prise off the latch using a thin piece of wood he found lying about in the garden. Pete climbed through the window making sure that he did not upset any of the pots that were on the kitchen sink. He then made his way to the back door in order to let John Lennon into the house.

- *"Whoopee,"* exclaimed John, *"this is exciting, now I know how real burglars feel when they're out on the job and what swag are we after? A grotty old tea chest!"*

They both saw the funny side as they always did in such situations. They made quite a thorough search of the house but no sign of the tea chest could be found.

- *"I bet it's in the garage,"* said John.

- *"Sshh. I can hear someone walking up the pathway. What are we going to do?"* Asked Pete.

- *"Have a quick look from behind the living room curtain. But for goodness sake don't let anyone see you."*

Pete peered anxiously from behind the net curtain but to his relief it was only a salesman going from door to door.

- *"John, it's okay, it's just someone trying to sell something,"* Pete whispered back to John (who had been getting ready to make a dash for the back door), *"by the looks of things I think he's giving free samples of something that looks like a drink away."*

Rat a tat tat, went the door knocker.*"Try the flipping bell,"* thought John as he plucked up the courage to answer the door.

- *"Good afternoon sir. I was wondering if your mother or father were presently at home?"*

- *"Nah me Mum's dead and me father's in the clink."* said John cheekily, yet at the same time in a manner that demanded pity.

- *"Oh I am very sorry to hear that."* said the salesman.

- *"What do you want to know for anyway?"* asked John who was starting to enjoy this interlude.

- *"Well we've launched a new drinks product you see. It's similar to Coca Cola and we're giving away free samples. Have you any brothers or sisters?"*

- *"Oh yeah. I've got three sisters and four brothers and me Uncle Herbert looks after us."*

- *"Well here are seven cans of our new cola for you all to try and if you could fill in the questionnaire sheet stating whether or not you like it. I will call again in a weeks time to collect them."*

- *"That's jolly nice of you - ta very much."* With that John grabbed the cans of cola from the amazed salesman and shut the door quickly in his face.

The two sat down for a while, feeling quite pleased with themselves over their handling of the situation, culminating in a most profitable seven cans of drink.

- *"He could have brought us some cans of beer!"* laughed John as he glugged down two cans of drink thirstily.

- *"What's that saying?"* said Pete as he lounged around on the sofa in Bill Smith's living room, *"never look a gift horse in the mouth."* Pete could see John didn't quite catch the drift of what he was trying to say. *"In other words Lennon, don't blinkin' moan when you get something for free."*

- *"What did we come here for anyway? I've forgotten."* said John, playing the game as always.

- *"The tea chest. I don't think it's in the house. It must be in the garage."* replied Pete.

- *"What's the time?"*

- *"It's 3:45 - Flipping heck! Bill Smith will be home from school shortly. We had better get the chest and head back."*

With that they put their empty cans in the waste paper bin and went outside to look for the chest. They eventually found it in the garage. They checked that everything had been left as they had found it, even leaving the kitchen window slightly ajar and made their way to the 61 bus stop carrying the tea chest.

- *'Hey I just had a thought,"* said John as they boarded the bus, *"we went to all that trouble leaving the place as we found it and yet we left empty cans of cola in the bin."*

- *"Ah don't worry, it's not like you to be so concerned, you sound more like me."* said Pete. *"Anyway, they won't have any evidence as no one saw us apart from the salesman."*

- *"What if the salesman calls back in a weeks time for the questionnaire forms?"*

- *"We'll sort that problem out if and when it comes."* said Pete who had had enough trauma and excitement for one day.
- *"Come on here's our stop, lets get off the bus and head home. If we're late I'll be under cross examination from you know who,"* said John (referring to his Aunt Mimi).

- *"Okay. Here, you take one side and I'll take the other."*

With that the pair landed on the pavement with the tea chest intact. It was a short wait for the 72 bus and the two parted company towards their respective houses as soon as the tea chest was safely back at it's home in Nigel Whalley's house.

Later on that evening Ivan Vaughan called around to John's house and informed him that I had agreed to take over full time as the tea chest bass player in the Quarrymen skiffle group.

The Jammy Hartley Incident

Saturday Early April 1957: Time - 12:30 p.m.

The Quarrymen skiffle group had arranged another practice session. It was early spring and the group had only been together for a few months. We had arranged to meet that Saturday afternoon at Eric Griffith's house.

Eric's house was situated about ½ a mile away from Woolton village in South Liverpool. It was a convenient location for a practice session for the Quarrymen as most of the group lived close wo Woolton Village, furthermore we would have the house to ourselvesthis particular Saturday as Eric's mother was out at work that day.

It was springtime in the south of Liverpool and the weather was unusually warm for so early in the year. John Lennon, Pete Shotton, Nigel Whalley and myself had all arranged to meet at Jo's Milk Bar in Woolton Village at 2 p.m. Eric Griffiths (our second guitarist), had arranged to meet us at his home.

We chose the Milk Bar as a rendezvous because it was so centrally placed and we all enjoyed the strawberry milk shakes they sold there; but the main reason

—Jo's Milk Bar: Hang out for Lennon & the gang: now a pet store..—

was that the proprietor - who we all knew as "Jo" was a rather attractive lady in her mid thirties and she always made a fuss of us whenever we popped in. I had decided not to bother collecting the tea chest from Ivan's house because for practice purposes it was not really required, as all I had to do was keep the rhythm of the particular song they would be performing. I didn't have to learn any chords or keys, my main input in these practice sessions was to give vocal support to John Lennon. On this occasion we had decided to try out some vocal harmonies, rehearsing such songs as: "Bye Bye Love" and "Dream" by the Everly Brothers, which had made such a big impression on us. I therefore decided after cycling up from my home in Wavertree to leave my Raleigh Rudge bicycle at Ivan Vaughan's house in Vale Road and walk into Woolton Village to meet the rest of the boys.

I called in at Ivan's at 1 p.m. I knocked loudly on the door and Ivan's mother appeared after about 5 minutes.

- *"Len, if you want Ivan he's in the back garden doing some chores for me. I'm afraid he won't be able to come out this afternoon."*

With that I parked my bike inside the driveway and made my way through to the back garden. Ivan, who had been a firm friend for about four years now, was on his knees weeding the flower beds.

- *"Hi there Ivy. Do you want to come along to the rehearsal this afternoon at Colin's house?"*

- *"Len I'd love to come along but can't you see I've just got too much to do? I promised Mum I'd dig the garden over and then I have a lot of homework to do. How's the group getting along?"*

- *"Well you know that I'm on the tea chest now that Bill Smith has been kicked out. I quite enjoy it although it is pretty hard work. I keep getting blisters on my hands."*

- *"I know, it's hard work. Before you and Bill Smith played it I used to and it gave me blisters. You need to wear a glove."*

- *"Thanks for the advice Ivy but I had already fathomed that one out. I wear a glove when I'm playing now. By the way Ivy, anytime I don't turn up to play you're welcome to take my place for me."*

- *"Yeah I know that Len. Thanks, but I'm not really that keen on performing. I only do it for a bit of fun, you know I can't sing, not like you anyway. You have a good voice and John needs your help."*

- *"Point taken. Anyway, keep up the good work. Is it okay if I leave my bike here because we're all meeting up at Jo's Milk Bar and then walking down to Colin's."*

- *"Of course you can. You'd better put it in the garage though, just to be on the safe side."*

With that I put my bicycle in Ivan's garage, said farewell and sauntered off down Vale Road, past Pete Shotton's home, turned left into Linkstor Road and down to Quarry Street.

I had a pleasant feeling as I walked up the hilly Linkstor Road. Looking into the small front gardens of the well kept semi-detached houses on that spring afternoon. I could see daffodils and primroses starting to burst into splashes of colour. As I walked enjoying all the sights of spring I thought how strange it was that this area around Menlove Avenue, Vale Road, Woolton Village and all it's surrounding roads where my friends lived had all become like a second home to me. This was like my adopted homeland now, I felt comfortable and at ease here and as usual when I felt happy, I began to whistle a tune. It was a song from

—Quarry Street shops where Lennon had street fight..—

"Seven Bride's for Seven Brother's" called "Bless your Beautiful Hide". Although I loved the new music of Elvis, the Everly Brothers and the like I still loved the musicals that had sprung up in the 1950's such as "Carousel" and this particular song reminded me of springtime.

I turned right at the top of Lincoln Road into Quarry Street and crossed over onto the other side. I looked at my watch (which had been given to me as a Christmas present) the time was 1:45 p.m. I reached into my corduroy jacket for a cigarette, there was just one left out of the packet of 5 Senior Service which I had bought the night before. I fumbled in my pocket looking for some cash. I needed 1 shilling and six pence for five cigarettes. I had about a shilling and ten pence, just enough for a packet of five and a milk shake. I stopped outside the newsagents in Quarry Street and popped in to buy my fags.

At the counter who should I nearly bump into but Pete Shotton's Mum who was busy settling her paper bill. I happened to be in front of her in the queue. In order to avoid her seeing me buying cigarettes I decided to make a point to the assistant serving behind the counter that I had forgotten to look for a comic on the newsstand and so let Mrs Shotton ahead of me in the queue. As I was perusing through the comics I was listening to the conversation she was having with the assistant.

- *"Oh, I didn't know there was a garden fête taking place. Where is it going to be held?"*

- *"At St Peter's church, it's going to be great fun; with the crowning of the Rose Queen and lots of sideshows. There's also going to be floats - you know, lorries decked out with flowers like a carnival."*

- *"Well, that'll be something to look forward to,"* said Mrs Shotton, *"I happen to know the caretaker, Mr Gillons and he never mentioned it to me. When is it planned for?"*

- *"Sometime in July. I can't remember the exact date."*

- *"Well my boy Pete has helped form a band called a skiffle group; the Quarrymen. His friend John Lennon is also in it."*

- *"Why don't you ask your Peter if the Quarrymen could take part in the fête? It would be good fun for them."*

- *"Yes thanks, I think I will."*

Mrs Shotton suddenly turned and spotted me.

- *"Why hello Len, I didn't see you there. Did you call on Pete? I think he's gone to meet John and Nigel in the village."*

- *"Hello Mrs Shotton, yes I know, I was just on my way to meet them."*

By this time I was next in the queue and just about ready to ask for my cigarettes. I wished she would go out of the shop before the assistant served me.

- *"If you see Pete tell him not to be too late for tea. No later than 5:30."*

- *"Yes okay Mrs Shotton I'll tell him. Goodbye."*

Just as Mrs Shotton was saying goodbye the shop assistant asked me what I wanted. *"5 Senior Service please."* I whispered. I looked up and to my relief she was outside the shop. Phew, I felt embarrassed and could feel myself going red in the face.

- *"Yes, can I help you?"* Repeated the shop assistant loudly.

- *"Just a pack of five Senior Service please,"* I said again, trying not to look guilty although my face was beetroot.

- *"That'll be one shilling and two pence sir."*

I wondered why I felt guilty about buying cigarettes and trying to hide the fact that I smoked from my parents and grown up people that knew me. Perhaps it was because I was still legally under age at 15 to buy cigarettes, but it had been made all the more embarrassing after the appearance of Pete's mother in the shop. I drew a deep breath to steady myself and headed towards Woolton Village. I looked at my watch, it was close to 2 p.m. and I quickened my pace as I headed down Quarry Street towards the village. It would take me about ten minutes if I walked quickly.

Well, well, so there's going to be a garden fête at St Peter's church. I seemed to remember John and Pete saying they had gone to Sunday school there when they were younger. What was the vicar's name again? Ah yes - Pryce Jones.

As I walked on down Quarry Street having lit up my second cigarette of the day my eyes strayed up one of the narrow side streets lined with neat terraced houses all built out of stone. It was like going back to the Dickensian age. I caught glimpses of the huge quarry where the sandstone rock continued to be mined.

This beautiful sandstone was the one that all the terraced houses were built out of and it was the same stone that was used to build the largest neo-Gothic cathedral in Europe; Liverpool Cathedral. This cathedral faced directly onto the rear of the Liverpool Institute of Education where I went to school. I couldn't help thinking that somehow everything was related; falling into some sort of plan. Now the skiffle group was called the Quarrymen. Hmm, now that I was one of them...

By this time my quickening steps, together with my wandering thoughts, had taken me to the end of Quarry Street and into Woolton Village High Street. As I turned to my left I looked across at the Woolton Swimming Baths. Youngsters were coming out spotlessly clean with their hair still wet from the water. I knew Ivan, John and Pete still went there to swim quite regularly although I never went with them because I had never learned how to swim and therefore never felt able to participate in this group activity.

The High Street was busy with bustling afternoon shoppers. The local shops were still the main source of merchandise in those days, there were no huge supermarkets with massive car parks to service them as yet, so the main street was always a hive of activity. I finally arrived at Jo's Milk Bar, which was situated right at the end of the High Street, past the Woolton Village Club on the right hand side of the street. That might be a place where we could play as a group, I thought as I passed. John, Pete and Nigel were already in the Milk Bar.

- *"Hi there Len,"* said John Lennon, who was perched on the edge of his stool sipping a milk shake, *"where did you leave your bike? It seems strange to see you walking."*

- *"I left it at Ivy's 'cos I knew you lot wouldn't be on yours."*

- *"Len, what would you like?"* This question was put by the rather attractive female owner of the Milk Bar, who we knew by the name "Jo".

- *"Oh, the usual, strawberry shake please."*

- *"Coming right up."*

She treated us as though we were part of her little brood and she always took an interest in our development as a skiffle group. Pete and Nigel were sitting at one of the small tables smoking and at the same time eating a large tub of ice cream topped with strawberry sauce.

- *"There you are Len that'll be just four pence."*

I handed the money over gratefully and started to relax and enjoy my milk shake, sitting on one of the bar type stools next to John Lennon.

- *"John where's your guitar, aren't you going to give us a tune?"* I asked. *"Jo might give us a free milk shake if she likes what she hears!"*

- *"Pete what did you do with my guitar?"* asked John.

- *"It's okay I left it in the corner - there, just by the front door."*

With a sigh of relief John Lennon, who had finished his milk shake by that time, picked up his guitar.

- *"Hey fellahs don't you think Jo looks like Doris Day? How about giving us a song Jo?"*

Jo responded with an embarrassed giggle. *"Ah, go on, you don't half flatter a girl. I thought you were going to say I looked like Marilyn Monroe! Anyway I can't sing, you're the entertainer John, go on, the stage is all yours."*

With that John picked up his guitar and started to sing one of Lonnie Donnegan's skiffle numbers, "Lost John".

- *"Lost John was standing by the railroad track,
Waitin' for the freight train to come back.."*

We all started clapping and Jo came out from behind the counter and started to dance. This was great, we were having a party! By this time Pete had got up from the table after finishing his ice cream and perched himself on one of the bar stools.

Jo was looking quite sexy and started to sidle up to Pete with her back to him and began to gently stroke his thighs. Pete Shotton went as red as a beetroot. By this time the few remaining customers had decided to leave; perhaps they felt that this was turning out to be a private party.

I suddenly realised that the time was about 2:30.

- *"Hey fellahs do you know we're supposed to be at Colin's by 2 o'clock for the practice?"*

- *"Ah shit, forget the practice, we're having such a good time,"* said John, who by this time was singing "All Shook Up", by Elvis Presley.

Nigel Whalley then called the whole thing to a halt. Jo laughingly gave us a free milk shake which we all gulped down quickly before we trooped out looking like reluctant heroes. We really didn't really want to go as we had been quite flattered; our egos inflated by the attentions of an attractive older woman.

We all trooped to the top of Halewood Drive. Suddenly we spotted a bus just about to leave the bus stop. I quickly ran on ahead, hopped on to the gangway of the bus, (which was starting to move slowly onward) and asked the bus conductor to stop as my friend, (John Lennon) was disabled. The conductor looked down the street to see Pete Shotton and Nigel Whalley seemingly helping this badly disabled youth; John Lennon, who was hobbling down the road.

The conductor looked on sympathetically and waited while the rest of the lads boarded the bus. It only took 5 minutes for the bus to get half way down the drive. At the stop we all got off, John Lennon still acting the part of the crippled young man, hobbled off the bus. As the bus started moving off John started to leap about, jumping up and down as the amazed conductor looked on. We arrived at Colin's house at around 2:45 p.m.. We were all by this time on a high note and ready for further fun. A serious practice session was the furthest thought from our minds as we entered Colin's house.

John Lennon, Pete Shotton, Nigel Whalley and myself all trooped into Colin's front room. Colin Hanton and Eric were already there but for some reason there was no sign of Rod Davies. There was however a friend of Rod's in the house and we were introduced. His christian name eludes me but his surname was "Hartley" so his nickname was automatically "Jammy" and I never knew him by any other name. There were also two young girls in the house who were undoubtedly members of John's unofficial fan club.

John Lennon and myself were very keen to try out the Everly Brothers harmonies and were going to attempt "Bye Bye Love" and "Dream". I could sense however that the general mood between Nigel, John, Pete and myself was not indicative of a serious time.

John was slouched in a comfortable armchair with his feet straddled over the arm of the chair. He had been careful to remove his shoes in case they should mark the chair; as a general rule when any of us were at anyone's house we always treated it with respect. Colin was set up on his drums in the corner, Pete Shotton and myself were on the settee. Eric was on the other single armchair next to John and Nigel Whalley was sprawled on the floor trying to think of any venues which were available where we could play. It didn't have to be for money, just somewhere that would have us.

- *"Len you'd better come here with me if we're going to try and sort these harmonies out,"* muttered John.

- *"Okay I'll change places with Eric then. Get over there Griffo!"* I said in a commanding voice.

Eric exchanged places with me so that I could sit closer to John.

- *"John, do you want me to do the high bits?"*

- *"Yeah, have a go. Let's try Bye Bye Love."*

Now my vocal range was quite similar to that of Lennon's but unfortunately I had not had the opportunity to listen to the song enough. You see, to get the words to any song one would have to play the record over and over again, writing the words down quickly. There were no such things as tape players where one could fast forward or rewind a tape, you couldn't do that with a record. John and I tried a few bars and then gave up.

- *"John, I don't feel much in the mood for a serious practice and anyway I don't know the words and you haven't written them down."* I protested.

John put his guitar down and Eric did likewise.

- *"Lets have a treat and a cup of tea,"* suggested Eric, who was starting to get rather frustrated that the practice session did not seem to be getting anywhere.
- *"Look guys,"* said Colin, *"if you want to smoke and have tea we'll have to go into the back room. If my Mum comes home and knows we've been in the front room* (this or "the lounge" was often the name used in those days meaning the best room) *she will murder me."*

We all agreed that we didn't want Colin murdered just yet as we needed him in the group. We therefore adjourned to the back room. This was used as a dinning room/occasional sitting room and there was a table that could be folded up to make more space. It was not terribly comfortable so some of us just sat on the floor on cushions while Colin went into the kitchen to make the tea.

- *"It's a pity we can't record some of our practices then play it back to see what we sounded like."* said Nigel Whalley.

- *"Well we could rig up a small speaker system using Colin's radio."* said

"Jammy" who was apparently an electronic whiz kid.

- *"Hey that sounds like a good idea,"* said John, *"it would save my voice and Len's. Okay Jammy, you do it."*

So Jammy rigged up the apparatus, with the radio in one room with a microphone and using a separate speaker wired up to the radio he then put the speaker in another room (the kitchen). The system meant that anyone could then switch on the radio with the intent of listening to a certain programme but on the flick of a switch it could then be used as a speaker system; with the person speaking from the adjoining room without being seen.

John, Pete and I looked at each other and large grins developed simultaneously on all our faces.

- *"I can see great possibilities here,"* said John and we all agreed, (we were all on the same mischievous wavelength). *"Pete, I'll go in the other room with the microphone while you flick the switch over to the P.A. system. Let Jammy think he's putting the radio on at a certain time and I'll announce something to do with Jammy over the radio, it'll scare the hell out of him."*

This sounded to us like a terrific idea and we all agreed to it.

Everyone was siting around feeling refreshed after our cups of tea and a cigarette but the time was now approaching 3:15 p.m. and no serious practicing had yet been done.

Meanwhile John Lennon had disappeared into the other room to get himself ready for his radio announcement.

Everyone else was lounging about, Eric started a tune up on his guitar. We were all joining in the skiffle chorus when in came Jammy Hartley who plonked himself down and immediately started singing. To keep Jammy occupied we all started to praise his singing; saying what a great voice he had and that he was destined to be a great pop star. Pete Shotton suddenly disappeared and gave John Lennon a signal to flip over the switch.

- *"Hang on fellahs,"* I said, *"I just want to hear the news."*

Everyone stopped singing. Suddenly there was an announcement coming directly from the radio's speaker;
- *"We apologize for the interruption to the scheduled programme of Mrs Doris Day but we have just received an important police message........."* announced

Lennon over the microphone.

I looked around at everyone's face. Pete and Nigel had their handkerchiefs at the ready; knowing that they would need them to smother their laughter. Eric, Colin and Jammy Hartley looked quite serious and attentive, none of them seemed to have realised what was going on as yet. The announcement continued;

- "............*There is at large an escaped lunatic believed to be in the Halewood or Woolton area of Liverpool. He was last seen heading towards the vicinity of Halewood Drive. Those residing in this area are advised not to leave their house under any circumstances and to lock all their windows and doors until he has been apprehended..........*"

Pete and I played along by going around the house, closing windows and locking doors. While we did so there was a pause in the announcement (probably while John Lennon was getting rid of a fit of giggles). As the announcement continued Pete and I went back into the room;

- "..........*Furthermore the police have warned that this person has a fervent hatred of anything or anyone that has a name linked to sweet things; such as lolly ices, ice cream, or even JAM. If these things are ever mentioned in his presence he will kill on sight. End of message.*" John by this time was hysterical.

- "*Oh ey Jammy you'd better be careful because your name is Hartley and Hartley's is a jam factory in Liverpool. Your life could be in danger!*" Said Eric Griffiths, who had by that time realised the joke and thought that he would play along for a while.

Just the sight of Hartley's face - the shock and then the sudden relief when he realised he had been the object of a practical joke was a sight never to be forgotten.

After that any thought of a serious practice session for the Quarrymen skiffle group was thrown straight out of the window and so we decided just to have some fun for the rest of the afternoon. Nigel Whalley wasn't too pleased however. Although Nigel enjoyed the fun just as much as anyone he took his job as our manager quite seriously and he pulled us up sharp.

- "*Listen if you all carry on like this you'll never get anywhere. We have to take these sessions more seriously. It isn't often that we get the chance to have somewhere to ourselves and Colin has been good enough to let us have the run of the place for a few hours and we have just wasted time.*"

It was about 4:15 p.m. and we all felt that what we'd been told was justifiable and made our apologies to Colin (Lennon as usual overdoing it, falling down on his face and apologising profusely).

- *"Look you can stay until 5 p.m. but by that time I want you to have cleared up all your fag ends, bottles and dishes and leave the place clean and tidy or my Mum will get to know that we've all been here and we'll never get to have the place to ourselves again."* said Colin.

- *"Okay Colin, we'll get around to that, don't worry we'll leave the place ship shape but I would like to hear Jammy sing again as I was so impressed earlier on."*

Lennon still had not had enough fun and knew there was more to be extracted from Hartley. I realised that in spite of Jammy having gone through the humiliating experience earlier he was still John's prime target for piss taking. We carried on in the same vein for the remainder of the afternoon, encouraging Hartley on his "stunning performances" on vocals.

This carried on until just before 5 p.m. then we all helped Eric to tidy up the house and left, feeling that it had been quite an eventful afternoon even though we had not progressed musically, we had entertained ourselves having had a great deal of fun. This to me was an essential element in the group, we had had a practice at fun making and I felt that as long as we continued to enjoy ourselves the musical side would eventually "come together".

John, Pete, Nigel and myself returned to Woolton Village, recounting amongst ourselves the hilarious events of the afternoon. It was now about 5:30 and we were in Vale Road outside Pete Shotton's house.

- *"By the way Pete, did you know that there is going to be a garden fête at St Peter's in July? I happened to be in the newsagents earlier on and met your Mum in the shop. She was talking about it and mentioned the fact that we (the Quarrymen), might be asked to perform."* Although I had mentioned it to Pete, John was listening and seemed quite excited at this.

- *"That sounds great Len. Pete can you ask your Mum about it and see if we can get hired?"*

- *"Yeah okay, look I'm late for tea. See you later."*

With that Pete Shotton dashed into his house for his tea.

- *"July? That's only a couple of months away,"* said John as we walked down Vale Road to Nigel's house.

- *"We'll definitely have to get it together by then,"* said Nigel as we arrived outside his house.

- *"We'll arrange a proper practice session for next week,"* agreed John as I collected my bicycle from Ivan Vaughan's house.

I had to knock on Ivan's door as I remembered that it was in Ivan's garage.

- *"Hang on a minute John while I get my bike,"* I called.

Ivan answered the door. *"How did the practice go?"*

- *"Oh we had a fantastic time, you should have been there,"* John related what we had done to Jammy Hartley.

John and I walked down Vale Road talking about the possible forthcoming performance at St Peter's. At the end of Vale Road I hopped onto my bicycle, said cheerio to John and cycled back home for tea. I arrived home just after 6 p.m.

St Peter's Church Garden Fête

Saturday 6th July 1957

This was the day that the Quarrymen skiffle group were to perform at St Peter's Church Garden Fête. It had been arranged by Pete Shotton's mother who knew the caretaker of St Peter's, Mr Gibbons.

It was an annual event on behalf of the church and involved a mini carnival of floats, consisting of five lorries making a procession through the streets of Woolton. Apparently we were to perform on five occasions that day. Firstly on the float then twice in the afternoon at 4:15 p.m. in the church field and then twice in the church hall starting at 8 p.m. that evening.

The week prior to this event we had arranged a practice/discussion at Eric Griffiths' house. It was Saturday afternoon, one week before the show. Present were John Lennon, Pete Shotton, Eric Griffiths, Colin Hanton, Rod Davies and myself.

- *"I don't really fancy going back on a lorry again. At least last time at Rosebery Street it was standing still. This time it's going to be moving while we're playing. We're going to look like right charlies."* John Lennon remarked as we all slouched around Eric's front room.

- *"It's not going to matter much, there will be that much going on that no one will notice what we sound like on the wagons."* I said, trying to reassure John.

- *"Yeah, I think that Len's right. All the kids will be interested in is seeing the guitars. Come on John, we'll have a laugh, we always do."*

- *"Yeah, yeah, great laugh. It was a great laugh wasn't it Shotty when those thugs were out to get me? Why is it always me that they're after?"*

- *"Because you're such an evil, dirty, smelly rat. That's why Lennon."* Pete said jokingly.

- *"Yeah Pete, you're probably right and I'm going to wear my evil, dirty, smelly check shirt next Saturday for the stinkin' show."*

- *"Is there going to be a microphone on the wagon?"*

- *"Nah, stupid question. We'll be bawling into nothing. You'll just have to sing a bit louder. We won't have a P.A. system."*

- *"In that case I'll just have to pick out the easiest songs that I can find. It'll have to do them. Anyway we're not getting paid are we Pete?"*

- *"Nah, you can have free food and cups of tea or bottles of coke. Remember, it's all for charity. Where's your compassion Mr Lennon?"* John ignored the remark.

- *"Len, with that haircut you look like a lumberjack, why don't you wear a check shirt like me?"*

- *"Well I suppose I could. I could borrow Wal's - it's red and black."*

- *"Red and black like a lumberjack. Hmm that could be the start of a song. Yeah okay Len. Mine's a light blue check, but so what? The rest of you lads can wear what you want. Now lets just check the song list."*

With that John Lennon did his usual practice of fumbling around for his bit of scrap paper.

- *"Oh by the way John, Ivan says he's invited his new friend from school to come and see us. I believe he's quite good on the guitar. Shall I tell Ivan that it's okay to bring the guy along?"* I asked.

- *"Look Len, anybody can come along, it's a free country. Tell this fellah to bring his guitar with him. He won't be playing with us though, we're very particular about who we have in the group. Nothing but the best musicians. Isn't that right Eric?"*

Eric was a bit startled at this and stuttered;

- *"Oh - err, yeah...nothing but the best. That's right John."*

- *"They're going to be crowning the Rose Queen as part of the show,"* said Pete, *"I wonder what she'll be like?"*

- *"Probably like the back end of a bus. That's typical of you Shotto, always thinking about sex. Anyway, you were crowned the king of the washboard recently weren't you?"* With that Lennon burst into his hyena like cackle. Then continued; *"Look fellahs, I'll go through the easy ones for the back of the lorry. Right are you listening? - 'Worried Men Blues', 'Maggie May', 'Railroad Bill' and 'Midnight Special'. We won't do any rock numbers, they're just not suitable for the back of a wagon. The rest we'll do when we're static."*

We all agreed to this and made arrangements to meet in Church Road the following Saturday at about 3:30 p.m. as this was where the floats were due to start their procession from.

The day itself arrived; the weather forecast was a cloudy humid day to start, brightening up with sunshine in the afternoon.

John Lennon woke up that morning at his usual time of 7:30 a.m. His immediate thought was about what sort of spectacle he would be making of himself that day, going around Woolton on the back of a lorry. He would have rather forgone this particular event, especially the open air sessions that put such a strain on his vocal chords. Never mind, at least we're in demand, he thought, consoling himself. Mimi was already up making breakfast in the kitchen so he made his way downstairs, lured by the smell of bacon being grilled.

- *"John - can you do the grass over this morning it's very long. You haven't touched it for weeks."*

- *"Yeah, yeah. Give it a rest Auntie. I've only just got up and you've already got work lined up for me."*

- *"Well, I've got no one else to do it and I'm relying on you."*

- *"I can do it this morning but I've got something on this afternoon and this evening."*

- *"It's not that skiffle group again is it? It seems to be taking over your life, no wonder the grass never gets cut. Still, it's better than being idle. Where are you playing? Not that other place where you got set on by those thugs? If it is then I really don't want you to go."*

- *"Nah, don't fret so much. Do you think I'd be daft enough to play there again? No, we're playing at the garden fête at St Peter's this afternoon."*

- *"Oh John, that's for charity isn't it? I am so pleased. Why didn't you tell me?"*

- *"I didn't think that you would be interested. You never usually are. Just because it's linked to the church you're all for it. You're always worried about appearances, that's your trouble."*

Mimi ignored this remark with a hint that John was calling her a hypocrite.

- *"Have you told Julia?"* (John's real Mum).

- *"Yes as a matter of fact I have."*

- *"And you didn't tell me?"*

- *"No because she shows more interest in the band than you do."*

The conversation went on for a while longer, with John contesting his Aunt's sincerity about his welfare. Afterwards John began to dutifully mow the lawn with the rather heavy steel man-powered lawn mower. He managed to mow the lawn by the side of the house, although he didn't get around to mowing the grass at the rear, this took him from about 10:30 till 12 noon. He was glad of the opportunity to get out of doors and expend some energy. Talking to his Aunt about his welfare bored him to death. He didn't see what all the fuss was about; he could understand if he was a criminal or part of a Teddy Boy gang that went around beating people up. Just then his Aunt called him in for lunch; it was nearly one o'clock.

- *"You're not planning to go this afternoon are you?"* asked John as they sat having their lunch.

- *"Well, I was thinking of going with Julia. You don't mind do you?"*

- *"I'd rather you didn't come. My nerves will be on edge."*

- *"Don't be silly, I've always wondered what you sound like with the band."*

- *"Oh please your self. Don't expect me to let on to you though."*

- *"I understand. Now finish up your lunch. You'll need the energy if you're going to be out all day."*

With that John disappeared to his bedroom to change into his blue checked shirt and collect his guitar as he had to be at St Peter's for 1:15 to meet the rest of the band.
Just across Allerton golf links, about 1½ miles away at 20 Forthlin Road, Allerton, Paul McCartney was also getting ready to go out to the garden fête at St Peter's church. He had been invited over by his new friend Ivan Vaughan to watch the Quarrymen perform.

Ivan asked Paul at school one day.
- *"Paul how do you fancy coming to the garden fête on Saturday. My friends are playing in the Quarrymen. Do you remember me telling you about John Lennon and his band?"*

- *"Yeah. Okay, I'll come. Tell you what I'll bring my guitar along as well just in case."*

- *"Yeah, bring your guitar as well. Call at my place at 2 p.m. The group will be on stage at the back of the church some time in the afternoon. I think they're supposed to start on one of the lorries, you know, the floats in a procession around Woolton, they leave from Church Road at 2 p.m."*

It was 1:45 p.m. and we had all managed to meet outside St Peter's. I had previously left my bicycle at Ivan Vaughan's place and with Pete and John's help carried the tea chest up to Church Road. Apparently we were to be on the last of the five lorries taking part. The first lorry was to carry The May Queen - a Miss Sally Wright, the other lorries were occupied by the local Scout group, the Youth Club and the Cubs and Brownies, all of which were linked to St Peter's

—St Peter's church: Church Road Woolton. View from Church Road.—

Church. The weather was warm and humid; Pete Shotton, the washboard player at that time was sweating already, as we waited on the pavement at the side of the rear lorry, waiting for instructions of when to get on board and set up.

- *"Pete, I had another set to with Mimi this morning."*

- *"Oh that is new! Why don't you tell me something different John, please?"*

- *"Shut up Shotto and listen. I told her that the group was playing here this afternoon and I think that she's coming."*

- *"So what? It's about time she took an interest."*

We were given the signal to board the flat back truck which had been decked with garlands of flowers for the occasion. The group of trucks were to be led by the band of the Cheshire Yeomanry; a brass band. We settled down to our positions on the back of the truck. The procession moved off very slowly as the church clock struck 2 p.m.

Reader please note: It has been written that John Lennon was drunk that day when he performed at the fête. However, I agree with Pete Shotton who recalls; *"He didn't have enough money to get drunk, even if we did like the stuff. We were drunk at the Rosbery Street celebration but I don't remember John being drunk on the day of the fête."*

- *"I just hope that we don't go down any steep hills,"* remarked Pete Shotton, *"or we'll all slide off."*

- *"I don't know where we're going,"* replied John as the procession gradually made it's way down Church Road to the High Street, *"but this hill is bad enough."*

Church Road has a gradient of about 1:4 as it slopes down towards the High Street. We decided that we would start playing when we had reached an even gradient. Meanwhile I decided to sit down on the tea chest and have a cigarette. We could see the morris dancers who were positioned about half way down the line of the procession.

- *"Hey it's a good thing that the brass band is at the front otherwise nobody would be able to hear us."* said Pete as we prepared to play our first number.

- *"I don't know whether that's such a good thing. If they were at the back we could have got away with miming."* said John.

John then started up "Midnight Special" as we got onto level ground. The Cubs and the Brownies were jumping on and off the lorries collecting money with their tins. We attracted quite a loyal band of followers as we slowly wound our way along the pre-planned route, along King's Drive and along Hunt's Cross Avenue. However, half way along the route we all decided to have a rest and I sat on the tea chest, the rest of the group sat on the back of the lorry, John was perched on the edge, playing his guitar.

- *"I've had enough of this,"* he said, *"whose idea was this anyway? It's all I can do to keep on my feet, never mind play the guitar and sing."*

The floats arrived back at the church at about 2:50 p.m. and we thankfully, as soon as the truck stopped, alighted with our gear. We were now in the top field where the Scout hut was situated.

- *"Thank goodness that's over with."* I said as we stored our instruments away in the Scout hut. *"When are we on next?"*

- *"It's supposed to be at 4:15 according to the programme,"* said Eric Griffiths, *"I think they're putting up a small stage in the bottom field."*

We all stayed in the Scout hut for a while, just glad of the chance to have a sit down on terra firma.

- *"I'm hot. Do you hear me Shotto? I'm not ever going on the back of a lorry again. No one could hear us properly and I couldn't get the chords right as the lorry was throwing me all over the place, my voice is getting hoarse trying to make myself heard."*

- *"I see John. Apart from that you're okay though are you?"* said Pete smiling, although he made sure that he wasn't within striking distance first. *"Cheer up John. Let's go and see the crowning of the Rose Queen. I think her name's Sally Wright. She might be the right one for you - you never know!"*

At that John laughed, the strain of not being able to show his real potential on the moving stage was dissipating now that the jokes began to flow.

- *"Don't bother. I've seen her and she's not your type John,"* I said, *"let's just wander about, you know; sign a few autographs, give a few locks of hair away...."*

- *"You'd have a job with that haircut."* remarked John light-heartedly as he eyed my crew cut hairstyle. *"I only hope that Mimi and Julia didn't see us while we were on the lorry. Hang on a minute, what's that noise?"*
We trooped out of the Scout hut into the fresh air in order to hear the voice coming through from the distant P.A. system.

- *"Hey it's Pricey. Well, well, it appears he's making some kind of speech. I hope it isn't one of his boring sermons."* exclaimed John (Pricey was the nick name for the priest, Pryce Jones).

John Lennon and Pete Shotton used to go to Sunday school at St Peter's when they were about 8 years old, although they were eventually barred as a result of their misbehaviour. John therefore was only too well aware of the priest's tendency to speak in long boring platitudes. On this occasion he was introducing the lady who was to crown the Rose Queen; a Mrs Thelwall Jones. I looked around me as Miss Sally Wright waited patiently to receive her crown. There were the usual side shows situated around the perimeter of the field. One involved a board to which playing cards were fixed. In order to win you would had to hit three aces with three darts. There was also a crockery stall where the aim was to knock down a row of six plates with six balls. There were the usual multitude of stalls with home made cakes, jams and biscuits for sale.

Once the crowning was over the side shows officially opened and people started to disperse from the main stage area where the Rose Queen had been crowned and we looked for fun in the surrounding side shows.

We joined the general mass of people wandering around, occasionally someone would recognize us as the skiffle group that played on the floats and say things like, *"Hey, enjoyed the music."* John would then reply, *"Oh did you like it? Good, thanks. We're playing again at 4:15. What time is it now by the way?"*

We had split into two groups John, Pete and myself in one and Eric, Rod and Colin in the other.

- *"John we'll have to be back up at the Scout hut by 4 o'clock. That'll leave us 15 minutes to cart all the gear down here and set up."*

- *"Yeah, okay Len. I think I'll have a go at smashing those plates. How much is it?"* He went up close to the stall and was squinting, trying to see the price of a game.

- *"John, I can see from here. It's 2p for six balls - you'll have to put your glasses on if you want to knock those plates down."*

- *"Okay."* With that he pulled two pennies and his glasses from his pocket.

He payed the money and was given six wooden balls in exchange. Unfortunately the size of the targets were reduced by only showing a ¾ of the plates.

- *"What do you get as a prize?"* enquired John.

- *"No prize, just another set of balls so that you can have another go."* Came the answer.

With that John let fly with all the strength he could muster and managed to smash four plates with his six balls.

- *"Phew, I feel better now,"* he said. *"Come on let's go, it's time to get the gear."*

The three of us went back to the Scout hut at the top of the field. Inside the others were already getting ready. Meanwhile the brass band was coming to the last tune in their afternoon repertoire; up until then the crowds had been entertained by the fancy dress parade, the most popular part of which was the under 7's group. Some were dressed as pirates and others as Snow White. Now it was time for another band; The Quarrymen skiffle group. We set ourselves up on the makeshift wooden platform which some people might have called a "stage".

John Lennon was at the microphone. He was centre stage and positioned right

—St Peter's field: Venue for Garden Fete gig for Quarrymen in 1957.—

up front. I was, from the audiences point of view, on his right and Eric Griffiths on his left. Rod, Colin and Pete were behind John who had asked me to get as close to the microphone as possible in order to help swell out the vocals. I therefore leaned as far across the tea chest as it would allow me to.

- *"Len, get a bit closer."* John said as he was about to start.

- *"I can't. Not with this thing."* I replied, referring to the tea chest with frustration.

- *"John, just get on with it, we've got a good crowd waiting for us."* Said Pete.

John then began to introduce us over the microphone.

- *"Is this thing on?"* He asked anxiously, looking around at the audience.

Someone from the crowd shouted *"Yes it's on"*. John was going to give a small introductory speech but decided against it as he felt unusually nervous performing in front of a "home" crowd, there were many people who knew him; relatives, Aunties, friends, enemies, who knows who might be in the audience? On the moving lorry we had only played skiffle numbers which were the easiest in our repertoire. Now John felt that we could show them what we could really do, performing what was becoming the love of his life; Rock 'n' Roll.

He therefore immediately launched into "All Shook Up" followed by "Blue Suede Shoes". Those in the crowd who had followed the floats were quite amazed at the change in Lennon's level of enthusiasm as he rasped these songs. The crowd quickly began to thicken and they drew closer to the stage as though drawn by a magnet.

- *"Keep going John, you've got an audience at last."* I said reassuringly and John looked at me grinned, he was starting to enjoy himself.

- *"This next song is dedicated to Pricey,"* he continued, referring to Pryce Jones, the priest.

The song was "Maggie May" which was the story of a Liverpool prostitute who walked the streets of Liverpool, namely Lime Street that were made famous as a haunt for prostitutes in the 1950s. The nerves had definitely gone, John was back to normal, obviously relaxed and wanting to shock and stir people into reacting (I don't think that Pryce Jones was in ear shot). While the song was being performed I could see Mimi and Julia weaving their way slowly through the crowd in order to get a better view. The weather was now very warm and humid.

I looked up at the clock high on St Peter's church tower. It was 4:45 p.m. *"Phew!"* I thought, *"still another half hour to go."* We were already sweating madly.

Meanwhile at the back of the crowd Ivan Vaughan's friend Paul McCartney was watching our performance with interest. He could see even from that distance that John was not playing normal guitar chords and that Eric Griffiths, the other guitarist was playing similar chords as John's.

Eric Griffiths said recently; *"None of us knew proper guitar chords. We played banjo chords instead, playing only the bottom four strings. It sounded okay though, good enough for skiffle."*

Paul drew a little closer in order to verify what he had seen from a distance. Yes it was true. He was amazed, John really didn't know how to play proper guitar chords!

- *"Well Paul what do you think? They're quite good aren't they?"* Asked Ivan of his friend.

- *"Yeah, the vocals are okay. I assume that that is John singing, but his guitar playing could do with a bit of attention."*

Paul was trying his best to convey the truth to Ivan without hurting his feelings, as he knew in what high regard Ivan held John.

- *"Well maybe you could show him a few things later on."* Ivan suggested. *"They'll be playing tonight at the village hall just across the way. Can you stay for that?"*

- *"Yeah I suppose so but it depends on what time they are going on. Where's the programme? That will tell us."*

Ivan handed Paul the programme, reading out the timetable as he did so.

- *"Look, it says that they are on again this afternoon and then again at 8:45 p.m. in the church hall.*

- *"Oh well then I can't stay for the late show,"* replied Paul emphatically.

- *"Well then you can come over to the village hall after the bands second performance for a drink and a bite to eat. They put on a good spread you know. I could introduce you to the band, anyway you already know Len Garry."*

Ivan was hoping that Paul's interest had been captured after he had seen John Lennon and was keen on Paul making his mind up to stay.

- *"Yeah, yeah okay Ivy you've persuaded me. I'll stay for a bite to eat. Meanwhile let's have a look around."* Paul said after a long pause.

The Quarrymen were coming to the end of their session. The clock sounded 5 p.m. The musical chime sounded clear above the sound of the music, the chatter, the laughter and all the noises of the summer fayre.

John wound up the session with "That'll be the Day" and made a little announcement stating that we would be playing again later on after the brass band. We then began to collect our instruments and took them back to the Scout hut for safe keeping. Some kind lady saw that we were dying of thirst and brought us out a tray with six glasses and a jug of orange juice for which we were very grateful.

Meanwhile Ivan Vaughan seeing John Lennon, sauntered over to the back of the Scout hut, excusing himself from Paul's company as he seemed intent on rolling a penny down the chute at one of the side stalls.

- *"Hi John, that was great."*

- *"Now, now Ivan, don't over do it. Pretty good would do."* said John as he reached for a cigarette, he reached the Scout hut with his guitar in his left hand.

- *"I brought my friend along from school."*

- *"Another friend from school? Oh yeah, I remember that you were bringing somebody. Where is he?"*

- *"He's over there by the side show. I asked him to bring his guitar but he hasn't brought it. I wonder if he forgot? Never mind. I've asked him to come over to the village hall later for something to eat."*

- *"Okay Ivy. Tell you what. Has he got his bike?"*

- *"Yeah why?"*

- *"Why don't you ask him to go back home and get his guitar, then we can have a jamming session in the hall later on."*

Ivan's eyes lit up with delight.

- *"Okay, that's great. I will."*

Ivan then left John, who by this time was stretched out on the grass beside the hut, cigarette in hand, staring up at the clouds that were drifting across the blue sky. The rest of us were glad of a rest and stretched ourselves out around our "leader". It was a bit like being on the bank again, lying back on the grass, deliberately not looking at one another, intent on our own thoughts.

John was glad that Mimi had insisted he had a decent meal at lunchtime as it was seeing him through the day without the craving for food he would otherwise have had by now. He hardly ever ate before performing as he seemed to get sufficient nourishment from an appreciative audience, he would be too absorbed in his performance to think of anything else, like a painter that would get "lost" whilst painting his picture.

Ivan meanwhile had caught up with Paul McCartney again.

- *"Paul, I've told John that you're here. I thought that you were going to bring*

your guitar and so did he. Why don't you cycle home. It's not far, get your gui-
tar and then you could meet us back at the church hall around 6 o'clock." There
was silence for a few minutes.

- *"I suppose I could but what for?"*

- *"John suggested that you might like to have a little jamming session before the*
evening show." another pause.

- *"Yeah okay, I'll do it."*

With that Paul retrieved his bicycle and cycled off home to 20 Forthlin Road to
collect his guitar.

It was nearing 5:30 p.m. I could see St Peter's church clock clearly from where
I was now sitting with my back resting on the wooden Scout hut. The other
members of the Quarrymen were already in the hut, I could hear the noise they
were creating whilst trying to sort out their instruments. I looked around and
there was John Lennon, still stretched out on the grass. He's asleep I thought.

- *"John, John! It's time we got our stuff together we're back on in a few min-*
utes." I shouted over to him.

There was a slight stir and then finally some muffled words.

- *"Okay, okay, don't worry. I'm awake now but I must have dozed off. How are*
your fingers? Are they still sore?"

I had been complaining about the blisters on my left hand, caused by playing
the tea chest bass.

- *"Oh, I'll be okay. I've got a glove with me and I'm sure that'll help."*

- *"Look we're only playing for charity. Why don't you take it a bit easier? You*
don't have to play it. You could get Ivan to have a go if you like."

- *"Nah, I'd rather carry on. Thanks anyway John.*

- *"What about your voice? Do you think it will last out?"*

- *"Well I'm going to take it easy for the next session because we've got to per-*
form again tonight. Anyway, most of the crowd are going now - look."

John called the Quarrymen together.

- *"Listen, we'll do the same session as we did on the lorry. The easier skiffle numbers, because I want my voice to last out. Is that okay?"*

There was general agreement as we were all feeling pretty tired and just wanted to finish off as quick as we could.

We made our way to the stage through the ever decreasing crowd. The police dog trials that had started at 5:15 were just coming to an end and we were to be the final attraction of the afternoon. Although still warm, there were dark clouds in the sky, hinting that there might be a chance of rain.

We carried out our performance as though we were switched onto automatic pilot, with hardly any enthusiasm we dutifully played and sang our way through our skiffle repertoire, keeping to the easy numbers as John had requested. By the time 6:20 p.m. came we had had enough. John gave a brief farewell and a reminder that we were going to perform at the village hall that evening. The small audience, mostly consisting of teenagers gave an equally small applause.

- *"Come on fellahs let's get this stuff over to the hall."* said John.

Needing no further encouragement we virtually ran from the stage, at least, we moved as quickly as our cumbersome instruments would allow us to. Ivan Vaughan came across to help as we were doing so.

- *"Listen, my friend Paul has gone home but he'll be coming back later on. I've asked him to bring his guitar with him."*

- *"What's that Ivy? Oh, your friend Paul. Yeah okay. We'll be in the church hall. Are you going home or coming with us?"*

- *"I've got to go home but I'll be back later."*

- *"Okay Ivy. Thanks for your help."*

With that Ivan Vaughan leaped onto his bicycle and went home for his tea. The Quarryman skiffle group marched along the path that bordered the graveyard of St Peter's into Church Road, across to the other side and past St Peter's school.

- *"I used to go to that school before I went to Mosspits Lane."* remarked Pete to me as we passed the building.

- *"Oh did you? I didn't know that it was a school. I went to Mosspits as well, didn't you know?"* We were now in the courtyard immediately in front of the village hall.

- *"John went to Mosspits as well didn't you?"* asked Pete, although John was nearly at the kitchen entrance of the hall and didn't seem to be paying him much attention.

- *"I believe so, so what?"*

We were now struggling to get past the crowd of people that were crammed into the kitchen, preparing sandwiches, laying out cakes and sausage rolls. A genteel old lady looked up at us as she stood, spreading "sandwich spread" on layers of white bread.

- *"Well done boys, you look tired - and hungry, go in. Store your instruments and then come and have a bite to eat."*

We all simultaneously replied, as though singing the chorus in one of our songs;

- *"Thanks very much we will."*

We stored our instruments in a corner of the hall and then went back into the kitchen to collect our plates of sandwiches and cake.

The time was 6:45 we had assembled ourselves towards the back end of the hall, away from the stage at the other end. We'd seen enough stages for one day; first a moving stage on the back of a lorry, then backwards and forwards to the stage at St Peter's field. We felt like blanking our minds from the fact that we were billed to go on stage twice again that evening. The musical menu for that night was to be; The George Edwards Band from 8:00 p.m. to 8:45 p.m. then we were on from 8:45 until 9:15. Our second performance was from 10:00 until 10:30, following the other band that would perform before us between 9:15 and 10:00.

Meanwhile Paul McCartney was chatting to his father at home in Forthlin Road as he was preparing to make his way back to St Peter's hall, calling at Ivan's on the way.

- *"Where are you off to son?"* He asked as he looked up from his crossword puzzle. *"You've been out all afternoon already."*

- *"Dad I've promised to go back to the Garden Fête. I told you about it yesterday, I went there this afternoon with Ivan Vaughan."*

- *"Oh Ivan, yes I know - nice lad. What was the fête like?"*

- *"Oh the usual side shows, the crowning of the Rose Queen and there was a dog handling show by the police training department. You know, the one just across from our back yard. You would have liked it."*

- *"And you're going back there now?"*

- *"Well there's this skiffle group playing called the Quarrymen and Ivan asked me to go and see them perform. I meant to take my guitar this afternoon but I forgot."*

- *"Why? You weren't supposed to perform with them were you?"*

- *"Nah I would just love the chance to play in a group Dad, you know that."*

- *"Yes I know that; you've made that very clear over the past few months, but you must not take for granted that everyone wants to hear you play. You've got to make it known that you're available but don't be too pushy, that puts people off."* said Paul's father rather firmly.

- *"Thanks for the advice Dad. Look I'm meeting them at about 7 p.m. What time is it now?"*

- *"6:30 p.m."* was the terse reply.

- *"Right where's my guitar, ah there it is. What's the weather like?"*

Paul looked out of the window; it wasn't raining. It was just as well for Paul as he did not have a cover for his guitar and as he was on the bicycle he could not put it inside his coat to protect it as he normally would have should it begin to rain.

- *"Cheerio Dad, I won't be late."*

- *"Good luck son and take care on that bicycle."*

Paul cycled off up towards Woolton with a sense of excitement that he had never felt before: he was looking forward to having the "jam" session with that friend of Ivan's - what was his name again? He thought for a moment, Lennon, that was it - John Lennon. He musn't be too pushy he thought, bearing in mind his Dad's advice as he cycled along. He had never thought of himself as pushy, he would just have to play it by ear and see how things developed. He had to call for Ivan first.

Back at the church hall, the George Edwards band were starting to set up on the stage, meanwhile the Quarrymen had split into two groups. I went out for a stroll with Pete Shotton and John Lennon as I gathered that our smoking in the hall was not very well received, though no one had actually said anything, we felt much freer outside in the open air.

- *"I fancy some chips, I don't know about you."* I said.

- *"Yeah, that's a good idea. Let's take a stroll down to the village."* The "village" was basically the High Street, about 100 yards down the hill of Church Road.

It was about 6:35 p.m., there was a thundery feel about the air.

- *"Did you realize that by the end of today we'll have performed five times in one day.? I wonder if that's a record?"*

- *"Just goes to show how popular we are,"* said Pete with a hint of a grin on his face.

By this time we had turned the corner of Church Road into the High Street.

- *"Oh what a lovely smell - Fish and Chips!"* I exclaimed. *"I think I'll get a large six penny bag."*

- *"Hey, hey steady on Len or you'll be getting fat. You need to keep that lean and hungry look, it looks better on stage."*

- *"Me! Get fat? You must be joking. My Mum says I've got hollow legs."*

This was an expression often used in Liverpool and meant that you ate so much without putting any weight on that the food you ate must be stored in your "hollow" legs. In the chip shop we had to wait in the queue for a while for our turn to get served. As we were being served Lennon leaned over the counter and looked longingly as the shop assistant piled up the golden brown chips (french fries) into a white paper bag.

- *"Salt and vinegar?"*

- *"Yeah, plenty of vinegar. In fact can I help myself to vinegar?"* Normally they would never put enough on.

- *"Alright help yourself, that will be six pence please."*

We made our way back to the church hall; it was now 6:55 p.m. Our fingers were greasy with eating our chips but we felt so much better with some hot food inside of us. After we had washed our hands in the small kitchen area, we entered the hall. Eric Griffiths, Rod Davies and Colin Hanton were squatting on the floor in the far corner. *"Where's Ivan?"* John asked.

- *"I thought he was bringing his friend here this evening?"* Eric looked up.

- *"He hasn't arrived yet, Paul has probably called for Ivan and Ivan has had to do some chores. You know what his Mum's like. Anyway where did you lot get to?"*

- *"Oh we fancied some chips so we walked down to the village."*

- *"Ah John, why didn't you tell me? You could have brought some back for us. We had to stay here to keep an eye on the stuff."*

- *"Look Griff, there's still time if you want to go and get some chips. Len, Pete and me can mind the gear."*

Eric did not take up John's offer as it looked like it might start to rain.

- *"Never mind,"* he said, *"I'll go and see if there's any sandwiches left."*

John Lennon meanwhile managed to obtain a few steel framed chairs with blue canvas seating and some of us sat down, John having previously retrieved his guitar. Just then the side door opened and Ivan breezed in, panting for breath as though he had just run a marathon.

- *"Hi there fellahs, look I've brought Paul along."*

The next figure to step through the doorway was Paul McCartney carrying his guitar. I think I was the only person in the group to look up as Paul walked over. John Lennon by this time had gathered another chair for himself and had his feet up, intent on replacing the broken string on his guitar. I knew Paul from the Institute and he recognized me.

- *"Hi ya, Paul glad you could make it."* I said.

Paul's face relaxed a little as he saw a face he knew.

- *"Hi ya Len."*

There was no response from Lennon, he didn't even look up. After Ivan had introduced Paul to the other members of the group he then approached John, who was still engrossed in tuning up the guitar string he had just put on. He looked up as if to say, "what are you bothering me for now?", it was an impatient sort of look.

- *"John - this is Paul...Paul McCartney, you know, I told you that I would bring him along."*

John took his feet off the chair and said simply;

- *"Hi Paul,"* then carried on tuning his guitar.

There was no shaking of hands, he didn't stand up to greet him, Paul just stood there.

- *"Hello John,"* he said in his polite manner, *"do you need any help with that?"*

John pulled up the now vacant chair.

- *"Yeah okay. Sit down."*

Paul sat down, took Lennon's guitar and handed him the guitar that he had brought along. Paul's guitar was left handed and so his guitar was strung the opposite way to that of a right handed guitarist, but that didn't matter when it came to the simple tuning of a guitar.

- *"Hey,"* exclaimed John as he inspected Paul's guitar, *"it's strung the other way round."*

- *"Yes, I play left handed."*

Paul then took a pitch pipe guitar tuner out of his pocket, playing the first in an open manner and at the same time blowing into his tuner.

- *"There, that's better. I'll just check that the other strings are in tune."*

The rest of us looked on admiringly as Paul showed his dexterity with the guitar.

"Hey fellahs" said John looking at us, *"he's good - we'll have to have him in the group."*

As I explained previously this was our joking response to anyone that ever showed musical talent rather than a serious or literal proposition. He was not as yet officially inviting Paul into the group. Ivan looked on happily with an expression which seemed to say; *"there you see, I told you he was good didn't I?"*

- *"Thanks Paul, it would have taken me ages to do that."* said John Lennon sincerely.

Now and then John would show true appreciation if anyone did anything for him. It all depended upon how the person did it. If Paul had helped John in a way that implied him wanting to "show off" John would instantly have cut him down with a sharp remark. However, Paul had helped John in a very low key manner that it made it evident to not only John but all of us that he was genuinely trying to help rather than showing off.

The time was now 7:30 and people were beginning to arrive for the show.

- *"Paul, what kind of pop music do you like?"* asked John, who was interested in finding out more about Paul's talent and taste in music.

- *"Well I used to like Lonnie Donnegan but now that skiffle is fading out I love the music of Elvis Presley, Eddie Cochrane, Gene Vincent, Little Richard......"*

- *"Hey,"* John interrupted, *"they're all the people I'm in to. My favourite record is Heartbreak Hotel. Do you sing as well as play?"*

- *"Yeah, I try, I had an audition for the cathedral choir once."* At that we all sniggered and Paul did not understand why we had all responded in that way. *"Did I say something funny?"*

- *"Nah, don't worry Paul, it's just that at one time Pete Shotton - Pete's over there, the one with the blonde curly hair,"* said John pointing to Pete, *"and I were choir boys once. Weren't we Pete?"*

- *"What's that?"* asked Pete as he wandered over.

- *"Paul was just telling me he was once in the cathedral choir and I was telling him about our time in St Peter's church choir. Do you remember Pete?"*

- *"Yeah, how could I forget? John and I were in the choir, we must have been about 9 or 10 years old. John would invent his own counterpoint to the hymns we sung and then we'd both end up on the floor in hysterics. Needless to say that we didn't last long."*

Ivan Vaughan, looking on, was so pleased at the way that things seemed to be going that he decided to spin things along a bit more.

- *"Paul, why don't you do your Little Richard impersonation, like you did at school last Christmas?"*

Paul looked a little embarrassed.

- *"Don't be daft Ivy, you're making it seem as though I came for an audition."*

However, John Lennon's interest in this cherubic faced, neat looking, slightly posey individual was growing fast.

- *"Yeah Paul, I'd love to hear you sing. Do a Little Richard number."*

Needing no more coercion Paul then gave us his rendition of "Long Tall Sally".

- *"Hey, that sounds just like him."* John said, *"I could never in a million years have done a Little Richard."*

- *"Why don't we get him to do it tonight?"* I suggested as I too had been very impressed.

- *"Don't be daft Len. You can't just ask someone that you've only just met to sing with the group."*

- *"I was just so impressed with that Little Richard impression that I thought he might be able to do that one song."*

Paul overheard as John and I were talking and interjected;

- *"Nice thought Len but I can't anyway, even if John asked me I couldn't do it. I'm only staying for a short while. I said I'd be home at a reasonable time tonight and in any case I've got no lights on my bike. By the way, what's the time?"*

The time was getting on for 7:15 p.m.

- *"What else do you know?"* asked John.

- *"Well, I know Twenty Flight Rock by Eddie Cochrane."*

Paul began to sing a few bars of the song. We were all amazed that he not only knew all the chords but also all the words to the song.

- *"How did you learn all those chords?"* asked John, who was anxious for more knowledge. *"Did you have a book?"*

- *"Nah, I've got a friend called Ian James at the Institute. He's far better than me and he taught me a lot. I could teach you if you like."*

- *"Well could you show me a few? Trouble is that with your guitar strung the other way it's difficult for me to follow. It would be good if you could draw a few diagrams showing the frets and finger positions."*

Paul looked at John and could see the hunger to learn in his eyes. He sat them down with a piece of paper and a pencil and drew out some bar chord diagrams for John to follow, making sure that it was for a right handed guitar player. Suddenly it was 7:30.

- *"Sorry chaps but I've got to go. Nice meeting you all, perhaps I'll see you again sometime. Coming Ivy?"*

With that he picked up his guitar and the two friends departed on their bicycles. It all happened so suddenly. John was left there trying to follow the diagrams on the scraps of paper that Paul had left strewn across the chair.

John Lennon spent the rest of the evening trying to put into practice the diagram of chords that John had left him, having had to wear his glasses for this exercise at least. He was tucked away from all the surrounding noise in a corner of the hall, away from the ever increasing congregation that had come to hear the George Edwards Band. Eventually Eric Griffiths joined him as he too was keen to learn proper chords.

- *"John you know we'll have to play the usual banjo chords for tonight's show."*

- *"I know that Eric,"* he snapped as he looked over his spectacles, *"I've learned more this evening than in all those guitar lessons we went to in Hunt's Cross. Do you remember what they were like when we first started?"*

- *"Yeah, I remember. What a waste of time they were! Let's have a look."*

With that the two of them, (for they were at that time the only two guitarists in the group), tried out the formations of the chords on their guitars.

—St Peter's village hall: McCartney auditioned for Quarrymen & met Lennon here.—

It was 8:30. I could hear people talking about the likelihood of a storm later on that evening. I can remember hoping that it would clear up before my cycle ride back to Wavertree. Up to now it had been an eventful day but very tiring and as a group, although committed to playing, we all wished that we could pack up and go home. All of us apart from John Lennon. I think that meeting Paul had wetted his appetite and by the time we went on stage for our first session at 8:45 he looked refreshed and seemed to have a new sparkle, as though he had had an injection of renewed optimism and enthusiasm as he played and sang through our usual repertoire that evening.

From my vantage point on the stage I could see somebody had a reel to reel tape recorder by the stage. John had completed fourteen songs, split between our two shows that evening. The first session started with "All Shook Up", "Be Bopa Lula", "Blue Suede Shoes", "Freight Train", "Hound Dog", "Maggie May" and "Railroad Bill". We finished just on 9:15 p.m. We had ¾ of an hour to recuperate. I could hear the rumble of thunder as the storm outside grew in intensity. I went outside for some air and a smoke; John and Pete decided to come with me. We stood outside pulling on our cigarettes, enjoying the breeze that had risen with the oncoming storm.

- *"Do you know John,"* remarked Pete as we stood outside, *"I've never heard you sound as good as you did just then. I know you're going to say that I'm not very musical but I could hear the difference I can see that something has happened to you. Even the skiffle numbers which I know you're not that keen on sounded good. You seem to have put more effort into them."*

- *"Pete's right John. I couldn't help noticing it as well."* I said.

John was silent for a few minutes, just enjoying his smoke.

- *"I guess someone took the trouble to share what he knew with me and it's just given me a little encouragement for the future that's all."*

- *"Oh I see, you're getting a little sentimental in your old age are you,"* joked Pete, who had never seen his life long friend in that light before.

- *"Don't be thick Pete. Come on I need a drink."* replied John, who seemed almost back to his normal abrupt self.

I said nothing. Our next session was from 10:00 p.m. to 10:30 p.m. and the audience had now begun to thin out. Many had gone early in an attempt to avoid the oncoming thunderstorm.

We were on stage again for our last performance of the day. John Lennon even surpassed the previous performance with his new found energy. He sang; "Baby Let's Play House", "Puttin on the Style", "Jailhouse Rock", "Worried Man Blues", "Cumberland Gap", "Midnight Special" and finished with Del Viking's "Come Go With Me". It was time to pack up our things and go home. John, Pete and I walked back to Vale Road, Pete helping me carry the tea chest which I was to leave at Ivan's that night. Fortunately the storm had abated.

- *"Well what did you think?"* asked John, directing the question to both of us.

- *"Think of what? Oh you mean how the day went."* Pete said, knowing all the while that John was referring to Paul McCartney. Then Pete answered the real question; *"I think he seems okay, he's pretty knowledgeable about chords, words and the like but I got the impression that he was a bit of a show off. You know, playing the guitar around his back like that."*

- *"Well I didn't think he was pushy. He was just showing me what he could do that was all."* John replied. *"If that's being pushy then I'm glad that he was."*

By this time I had arrived at Ivan Vaughan's house, we parked the tea chest around the side in the shed, which Ivan had said that he would leave open for me and I retrieved my bicycle. John and Pete were still having a discussion, whilst standing outside Ivan was waiting for me.

- *"Well cheerio fellahs. See you on the bank next Saturday."*

- *"Yeah okay Len. See you."* they replied and I cycled off home.

Pete walked with John round to Mendips: it was about 11 p.m. They stood on the corner of Vale Road and Menlove Avenue. It was where the two life long friends would always meet in the mornings before cycling to school. They were still talking.

- *"Pete?"*

- *"Yes?"*

- *"I was thinking of asking Paul if he wanted to join the group."*

John had been pondering and dwelling on this thought all the way back home from St Peter's. Here was somebody who would be able to help him to develop musically but he didn't want to make any hasty decisions and he also felt that he needed the support of his old friend.

- *"Well if I were you I wouldn't be too hasty about asking him. I mean he out-shines you on the guitar and to be honest he can sing songs that you would never attempt to sing, like Long Tall Sally. I mean, wouldn't it make you feel a little threatened?"*

- *"Threatened? Flippin' heck Pete! I'm not that complicated. I just want the group to make progress that's all and I think that he would be an asset. He could help me a lot, well we could help each other. I would be helping Paul because he's always wanted to be in a band."*

- *"Yeah I know John. Let's give it a couple of weeks though eh? Just see what develops, after all there's no rush is there?"*

- *"Yeah okay Pete. I think you're right. We'll leave it for now. Well, I'm off to bed. I hope Mimi isn't waiting up for me. I'm whacked. See you tomorrow."*

- *"See you mate, sleep well."*

The two friends parted. About two weeks later Paul McCartney had cycled up to see his friend Ivan Vaughan but he wasn't at home. Pete Shotton had just left his house to call on John Lennon when he saw Paul turning the corner of

Wal was a keen listener of jazz: **Bix Beiderbecke** and Jerry Roll Morton were household names to him.

- *"Anyway,"* I added, *"I'm only playing the thing for the opportunity to sing on stage."*

- *"Oh, now we're getting closer to the truth of the matter. You use that tea chest as a prop because you haven't got the nerve to sing on your own. Am I right?"*

At this remark, with my **Mum** and **Dad** looking on, I went bright red with embarrassment, knowing full well that Wal had hit a "bull's eye".

- *"Come off it Walter. Leave the lad alone. All he's doing is having a harmless bit of fun and at least he's keeping off the streets."* said Mum, trying to mediate a little.

Dad looked at the clock. It was 4:55 p.m. He quickly drank his tea, leaving his tea leaves on the side of his cup, as **Mum** would normally take these up and "read" his future in the leaves. However there was no time for this tonight.

- *"Phyl,"* (short for Phyllis), *"have you got my sandwiches? I've got to dash. Cheerio Len, take care of yourself. Bye Wal."*

With that he gave my **Mum** a goodbye kiss and ran for his bus which he caught at the corner of Lance Lane, in Heathfield Road. My Mum would then go into the front room to look out of the bay window, from which you could see the whole of Lance Lane. She would wave to my Dad just before he turned the corner of the road to catch the bus and my Dad would wave back.

Just then the phone rang. It didn't often ring because in the 1950's not many people had private telephones. I answered it.

- *"Hello Childwall 2936."*

- *"Hi Len, it's Pete. Listen, I've heard from Nige that you're playing at Wilson Hall tonight."*

- *"Yeah that's right, so what?"*

- *"Well I was thinking of coming along to see you because I missed Paul's debut with John. I wanted to be there but I couldn't make it last time."*

- *"Pete, you know that we're always glad to have you along- why don't you bring your washboard just in case?"* Pete laughed.

- *"Seriously though Len. You know what Wilson Hall is like. I don't want you to think that you're going to be on your own if any trouble does break out."*

- *"Why should any trouble break out?"*

- *"Because Rod and Willo are out to get John and they've been known to frequent that place. I don't think that they live that far from there, somewhere in the Garston area anyway and what's more they've got a load of mates as well."*

- *"Len, who's that on the phone?"* **Mum** called from the dining room, where she was clearing up all the tea things.

My hand automatically went over the mouth piece of the telephone.

- *"It's okay Mum, it's only Pete Shotton wanting to know when and where we're playing tonight."* I took my hand away from the phone. *"Pete, I think that we're due on at about 8:30 p.m. Don't start telling John about Rod. Just be there to keep an eye out for us, okay?"*

- *"Yeah, I'm pretty sure that I can make it barring accidents. By the way, how are you getting the tea chest to Wilson Hall?"*

- *"I've arranged to pick it up from Nige's place and then we're both going to carry it across the Golf Links to meet up with the others at Paul's place."*

- *"Okay I'll see you later on in the hall. Cheers Len."* With that Pete rang off.

I wondered why he hadn't offered to carry the chest with Nige. It would have saved me a journey. Never mind, at least he was going to be there later on. I was starting to feel a bit worried about the possible outcome of the evening. It was about 6 p.m. Mum had cleared the tea things and was in the kitchen washing up. My elder brother Walter could see the anxious look on my face.

- *"What's up Len?"*

- *"Oh nothing, don't worry. It was just Pete Shotton asking where we were going to play tonight."*

- *"Where are you 'playing' - I hate using that word!"*

- *"Wilson Hall, Garston."*

- *"Wilson Hall? That dump!"*

- *"Shh Wal, keep your voice down or Mum will hear you."*

- *"Listen Len, you know the types that hang around there, Teddy Boy gangs looking for a fight and that. I'd advise you to steer clear of that place."*

- *"We can't back out now. We'll just have to keep our wits about us. Anyway Pete Shotton said he would keep an eye out and let us know if he senses any trouble."*

- *"Do you want me to come along?"*

Wal by this time had just graduated to a brown belt in judo and was always throwing Dad and me around the house, practising the various holds and throws.

- *"Nah Wal, honestly, we'll be alright. Let's drop it. Here's Mum."*

- *"Look lads. I know that there's something going on. What are you talking in a whisper for? You can't fool me. I'm your mother!"*

I had to tell Mum where we were playing that night and that Teddy Boys might be a problem but didn't tell her any more details to avoid worrying her too much. I knew that she was worried anyway, I didn't want to add to her anxiety. I appreciated my brother's offer of help. I knew that although we didn't have much in common there was a brotherly concern that manifested itself in times of need. It was comforting. I wondered why it was that people always seem to draw together in a crisis. For example at funerals; sometimes you never see certain relatives for years and then they suddenly appear saying, "is there anything I can do?".

I looked at Mum, then at Wal and felt a sudden urge to give them a big hug. I went into the kitchen where Mum was finishing off wiping over the sink, came behind her and gave her a big bear hug. She turned and smiled.

- *"Now, what are you after?"* she asked.

Although I wanted to give Wal a hug I refrained from doing so, prevented by masculine pride. It wasn't the normal thing for men or boys to hug one another. Looking at my Mum's face just afterwards I could see a little tear in the corner of her eye. There was love in this family, it was just the inherited, stubborn "Garry" streak that stopped it from being demonstrated and I was just as bad. I looked over at the clock. It was 6:30 p.m. I reckoned that I would have to leave by 6:45 at the latest to give me enough time to cycle to Nige's, collect the tea chest and then walk over to Paul's house where we were expected at 7:45.

- *"I know, let's all go into the front room and put the fire on for half an hour while Mum plays the piano."*

I could sense that we all needed cheering up and offered this suggestion in order to change the tone of the conversation.

- *"I'll make a pot of tea,"* I added. *"Come on Mum, I haven't heard you play for ages. You always used to play whenever Uncle Jack came round."*

My Dad's brother Jack had a good tenor voice and used to come quite regularly to our house, usually on Sunday evenings. We would all gather in the front room, Uncle Jack standing beside the piano, with Mum sitting at the piano singing songs like "Come Back to Sorrento". I used to enjoy those evenings. Mum agreed to my suggestion and started looking in the piano stool for her sheet music, while Wal lit the fire and I went into the kitchen to make a pot of tea. Thus for the next half hour Mum played the piano, including my favourite piece "Clare de Lune" by Debussy. It seemed to sooth all the tense nerves in my body and from the look on Mum and Wal's face it seemed to have the same effect on them too.

Suddenly it was 6:50 p.m. then it was a mad rush to get all my things ready. It was just as well that I didn't have to worry too much about my appearance tonight as there wouldn't have been time. We had agreed as a group not to be over concerned about dressing too smart, given the type of venue we were going to. The weather forecast for the evening was dry at first but with the chance of rain later. At the moment it was dry. I wheeled the bike out of the garage, said my farewells, buttoned up my jacket as it was quite a chilly night and then set off on the now familiar route to Vale Road

I arrived at Nigel's at 7:15 p.m. as planned.

- *"Nige, I need to leave my bike here is that okay?"*

- *"Yeah sure, put it around the back and I'll lock the gate. Get the tea chest while you're in the shed."*

- *"Okay."*

With that I wheeled my bicycle to the back of Nigel's house and brought out the tea chest.

- *"Ahh eh Nige, it's getting a bit tatty isn't it?"*

- *"Yeah, I meant to paint it up a bit but I haven't had the time. What time is it now?"*

- *"7:20. Come on, we've got to walk across the Golf Links carrying this. Why haven't you ever considered putting wheels on this thing? It would be a lot easier."* No response from Nige.

The two of us grabbed a side each of the tea chest and set off across Allerton Golf Links. It was quite dark but it was a familiar route as "the gang" had often come down this way to play a game of "Roofball".

- *"Hey Nige what do you think of the new lad in the group?"*

- *"Oh you mean Paul? I don't really know what to think. He seems okay but I can't really see him being part of the gang. I think that his Dad keeps him on a pretty tight rein."*

I decided to change the subject.

- *"Shotton rang me tonight."*

- *"Oh yeah, what about?"*

- *"Well, it looks as though Rod and Willo might be after John and Pete thinks they'll be at the show tonight."*

- *"He's dead right. I'm pretty sure that they will. But Shotto can keep an eye out for them. He is coming isn't he?"*

- *"Yeah he said that he would but you know what Pete's like. Everything can change at the last minute with him."*

At this point in the conversation we had arrived at the mid way point up the path that led across the links; there were no street lights so even though we knew the path pretty well we would occasionally stumble across stones and bricks, sometimes actually dropping the tea chest, which had already been looking tatty.

- *"Hey, there's the place where we used to play Roofball."* I said.

Just as I did so the park policeman appeared in view from the corner of the building.

- *"Ay ay and where are you two lads off to with your swag?"* (Swag meaning stolen goods).

I could see he was referring to the upturned tea chest with the broom handle sticking out. Although time was getting on Nige and I couldn't resist the opportunity for a laugh.

- *"And also lads why were you looking up at that roof so intently? You must admit that it does look a bit suspicious you two carrying that box thing and then I catch you staring up at the roof of that building."*

We had to agree that it did.

- *"It's not what you think Ossifer,"* I joked, *"you'll never believe this but we're actually musicians in a rock band and we're on our way to meet the rest of the band because we're performing tonight."*

The policeman looked at us and thought for a few moments. Then he looked again, this time noticing the word "Quarrymen" on the tea chest.

- *"Is that the name of your band? Where did you get that from?"*

I looked at my watch. We were supposed to be at Paul's for 8:00 and the time was 7:45 already. The policeman was still eyeing up the tea chest.

- *"You still haven't explained what the chest is for. Until you give me a satisfactory answer then I'm afraid that I can't let you go."*

Nige by this time was getting worried, bearing in mind that his father was in the police force. If Nige ever got into any sort of trouble with the police then there would be hell to pay. Nige decided that it would be better to make another attempt at explaining.

- *"It's not really a rock band, we're a skiffle group. Haven't you ever heard of Lonnie Donnegan?"* The policeman looked blank. *"Well anyway this box here is actually a musical instrument. We're carrying it upside down, look."*

Nige turned the chest the correct way up, put the pole on the side, attached the string and did a demonstration of how to play it.

- *"Well I never. I've seen some peculiar things in my time but nothing quite like this. You mean you actually go on stage and play that thing?"* He shook his head again in astonishment.

- *"Now officer, is that explanation enough? We really have to go."*

- *"Ah go on then. You must be telling the truth to come out with an explanation like that. They say that life is stranger than fiction. Best of luck lads."* With that he disappeared back into the darkness.

- *"Come on Nige, we'll have to run for a while."*

- *"Why do we always get the best jobs?"* Nigel gasped as he started running, carrying the chest.

We finally arrived at 20 Forthlin Road at 8:15 p.m. John and Paul were already there.

- *"Where did you two get to? We thought that something had happened. The "hound of Allerton" might have got you or something!"* Said Paul light heartedly.

- *"Have you got a cup of tea Paul?"* I asked.

Paul went into the kitchen and put the kettle on. I then related what had happened to Nigel and myself. John and Paul burst out laughing.

- *"Hey Nige you'd have been in the shit if that copper had taken your name, your Dad would have taken the strap to you again. I can just picture that fellah's face when you explained to him that that thing was a musical instrument."* said John grinning widely.

- *"Okay, okay,"* I said, *"don't go on John. "* I felt a surge of embarrassment because my instrument was the cause of such hilarity. *"Look guys that's enough. What have you two been doing while we've been struggling to get here? I hope you've done some practising and got the song list sorted out?"* I was getting more and more annoyed as this episode was dragging on.

- *"Yeah, yeah, don't worry Len. Paul and I have got it all sorted out. Haven't we Paul? Paul! Paul! I said haven't we Paul?"*

Paul McCartney looked up with a wry smile and paused.

- *"Tonight will run just like clockwork. I am going to give the audience the best rendition of 'Guitar Boogie' that they have ever heard this side of Garston."*

- *"Hey this is a new twist,"* I said, *" Paul just cracked a joke he must have a sense of humour after all. John, shall we have him in the group?"*

John was enjoying the banter as ever.

- *"Yeah, we'll give him another try and if you don't get it right this time Jimmy...",* Jimmy (James) was Paul's first name, *"then..."* John waited to see the expression on Paul's face, *"then we'll....",* again a pause, by this time we were hanging on John's next words, *" ...then.....we'll have to send him for some more guitar lessons!"*

Paul joined in the laughter and at that we were all back to normal.

- *"Hey lads, look at the time. It's nearly 8:30. We'll have to go now we still have to catch the bus."* Nigel Whalley reminded us, trying his best to act like an efficient manager.

We suddenly sprang into action. John and Paul grabbed their guitars and Nige and I took a side of the tea chest each. We then headed towards the 86 bus stop in Mather Avenue. It was only about a twelve minute ride to Wilson Hall but the busses were not very regular at that time of night, so we had no idea how long we would have to wait.

In actual fact we waited about 5 minutes before the 86 came by. The one moment I used to dread when I was going to these venues was when we were travelling to and from them by public transport, the times when a surly conductor would take a good hard look at the tea chest and say to me emphatically, *"Don't think for one moment that your bringing that thing on here".* If this did happen, (and it did happen more than once), I would have to shout up to John and Paul, who by this time would be on the top deck entertaining the passengers. I would have to call upstairs and explain to them that the conductor wouldn't let me on. Sometimes the conductor would give way after a little more persuasion from John.

Tonight, thank goodness, there was no problem. In fact he was a rather genial bus conductor, saying as we climbed on board;

- *"Where are you playing tonight lads? If it's the Liverpool Empire then you're going the wrong way."*

It makes it so much easier when people are pleasant. Nige and I stowed the chest

was about to lose my temper and tried to reassure me.

- *"Come on Len, we need you,"* then after a pause he added, *"honest."*

The very fact that John had added the word "honest" to his comment did not reassure me completely but it helped.

We finally arrived at Wilson Hall, or as it was otherwise known - "the blood bath"(as a result of it's bad reputation for fights). We made our way to the side entrance by which time it was about 8:45 p.m. It had taken us about 30 minutes to travel half a mile. We were due on stage at 9 p.m. and I believe we were the only live performers that evening, the rest of the evening's music coming from a juke box. We were all gathered in the back room apart from Eric Griffiths and Colin Hanton who as usual were running later than we were.

- *"Where's Eric and Colin?"* asked John.

I answered him in a posh voice;

- *"Why didn't you know John? They are arriving by car. Once they have arrived there will be a special announcement made to inform us that they have entered the building."*

- *"Cut the crap Len. We're due on any minute."*

John was getting jumpy by now. I think that he was aware that Rod and Willo could show up that night but was keeping tight lipped, not wanting to show that deep down he was feeling very vulnerable.

- *"John, have you seen the state of this?"* I said, pointing at the tea chest.

Some of the aluminium edging was starting to come away and the black paint had scrape marks all over it.

- *"Ah don't worry. You'll be at the back of the stage anyway, just like the line up at Clubmoor Hall. No one will notice from that distance, you worry too much."* It was 8:55 p.m. the juke box music in the hall had stopped. Eric and Colin suddenly came staggering through the side door.

- *"Sorry we're late but the guy giving us a lift was late. Anyway, we're here now so the show can go on."* said Eric breathlessly.

John was tempted to let fly verbally but was secretly relieved that despite all the obstacles the band had made it with a couple of minutes to spare.

- *"What's the crowd like?"* asked John. *"I hope that those two fellahs Rod and Willo aren't here."* This was the first time that John had publicly declared his anxiety.

I took a peek from the stage door. Someone had started the music up again; Little Richard's "Long Tall Sally" and a crowd of teenagers were jiving away to the music.

- *"Any nice one's there?"* Asked John.

- *"Nah, only scrubbers"* (meaning ordinary looking girls), *"nothing to write home about."*

John and Paul were having a quick look through the song list now. The show was running late and Charlie McBain, the owner and promoter, stuck his head around the door.

- *"Aren't you lads ready yet? You should have been on stage ten minutes ago and where's your smart outfits gone? I know what you're going to say - it wasn't worth dressing up for a place like this. Well that doesn't wash with me. Next time - if there is a next time - try to look smarter."*

- *"Hang on Charlie"* replied John, *"if we told you the trouble that us lads have had getting here on time you'd never believe it. We've got to use public transport you know, not like you in your fancy car."*

- *"Hey, watch it Lennon, he who pays the piper calls the tune, remember that. If you're not on stage within five minutes, I'll repeat that; five minutes then I'll cancel the show."*

With that ultimatum we quickly scrambled, just as the World War II pilots did when they scrambled for their Spitfires. We were on stage in double quick time. The music from the jukebox was still playing as we set up on stage, virtually unnoticed by the crowd. It was to be Paul's second public appearance with John. John and Paul were setting themselves up by the microphones and I could hear them say jokingly;

- *"I don't know what I'll do when they start throwing their knickers at me."*

- *"With the state of this lot your welcome to them."*

Then we started up. The first number was "Twenty Flight Rock" with Paul as lead vocalist. Every eye was turned towards the stage. The song went down well with the audience and we received an enthusiastic round of applause. Next it was John's turn with "That'll be the Day". If I remember correctly this was the very first song that he learned how to play on the guitar. I could see a change in the expressions on the faces of the crowd as John began to sing. It was as though John had the ability to command that they pay attention, all the usual chatter that had continued during Paul's singing stopped. In spite of the poor quality of the P.A. system and our poor quality instruments his powerful nasal rasp and stage presence seemed to carry us through.

Things were going quite well I thought as I viewed the performance from the back of the stage. My fingers were beginning to get sore and the blisters that had appeared a few weeks ago started to get bigger. I reached for the glove which I usually kept in my left pocket quickly, so that no one would notice. To my relief I managed to find it and during a short interlude between songs I quickly slipped it on to my left hand. There was no way of knowing whether or not the bass could be heard by the audience as there were no sound monitors and I didn't have my own microphone but I had to put these thoughts to the back of my mind as Paul announced over the P.A. system his second rendition of "Guitar Boogie".

This time Paul had done his homework, he was more confident and relaxed, perhaps part of the reason was the freer atmosphere in this particular club but equally importantly he had also had a bit more time to fit in with the group musically and more importantly, on a personal level. His rendition was faultless. We continued with the performance with no major hiccups apart from John Lennon's 6th string breaking on the last number. John's reaction to this was just to ignore it and play on until the end.

- "*Phew*" we all sighed with relief that we had finished our first session. We were all ready for a drink and a smoke. I looked into the crowd to see if I could spot Pete anywhere but there was still no sign of him and it was now 9:40 p.m. Colin Hanton had his usual supply of drink with him and shared it with John.

- "*Ah, that's better. Anyone got a ciggy?*" He asked.

I handed him one of my Senior Service cigarettes from the three remaining in the pack.

- "*Any sign of Pete? I thought you said that he'd be here?*"

- "*I've had a look around John but I can't see him.*"

We settled ourselves in the little room back stage and began chatting about the performance when the door suddenly swung open and a mass of blonde curly hair appeared.

- *"Hi there fellahs, how's it going?"*

- *"Pete! Cor it's good to see you,"* said John, *"come in, how long have you been here?"*

- *"I've only just arrived. My brother Ernie is back home so I had to spend a little time with him."*

Ernie Shotton, Pete's elder brother by a few years, was a merchant seaman and Pete had a great deal of affection for him. Ernie would generally bring home presents for the family, including large packets of "Capstan Full Strength" cigarettes for Pete.

Pete Shotton was particularly interested in seeing Paul McCartney and John Lennon performing together. He had had to pay the admission fee of two shillings and sixpence, rather reluctantly, having failed to gain entry in spite of his insistence that he knew us all.

The second half of the show went as planned and we all received a favourable response from the audience. After it was all over we trooped back stage and began packing up. I by this time had decided to ask John and Pete to take the tea chest home with them back to Woolton Village, as Nigel Whalley had disappeared half way through the evening and could therefore not help me to carry it.

- *"Pete and John, would you do us a favour and take the tea chest with you? If I have to hike it all the way to Woolton Village it means that I'll have to get two buses home."*

- *"Yeah no problem Len, we'll do that,"* Pete replied.

- *"Any sign of Rod or Willo?"* asked John.

The names Rod and Willo were our shortened versions of Rodney Johnson and George Wilson, both of whom came from the Woolton area of Liverpool. They would also usually hang around with two or three other tough looking guys.

- *"No I haven't seen them, I think we'll be okay."*

- *"Paul, can you and Len take my guitar. You could leave it at Paul's place, is that okay Paul? Cos' we've got the tea chest."*

- *"Hang on a minute,"* I said, *"we've not been paid yet. I wonder where Nige has got to? I'll bet he's run off with our fee!"* I said jokingly. *"Let's go and see Charlie."*

I knocked on the door of the little office from which the owner ran his "little emporium". Paul came along to offer me support. He eventually opened the office door.

- *"Come in, come in. I suppose you want paying?"*

- *"Well, as much as we enjoy performing we don't do it for nowt."* I replied, trying my best to be assertive.

- *"Where's your manager disappeared to? What's his name again Nigel Whalley? I'm supposed to give him the fee."*

- *"I think he's gone off home sick."* said Paul quickly.

Although he didn't realize it at the time there was actually a large element of truth in his reply. In fact Nigel had had an asthma attack and had to go back home in order to get his inhaler which he had forgotten. He had therefore disappeared half way through the performance.

- *"Well here's what I agreed with him."* continued Charlie as he handed over five ten shilling notes.

We took the notes, went back to the others and handed everyone a ten shilling note each. Then Paul, John, Pete and myself walked towards the bus stop. The 86 bus stop from where Paul and I would be catching the bus was fortunately next to the one where John and Pete were getting their bus home, we therefore felt fairly secure waiting together. The 86 was the most frequent bus service and came along first. Paul and I began to board the bus, waiting in the queue for the other passengers to alight. I turned to see John and Pete standing there, either side of the tea chest bass.

- *"I hope you have less trouble than I did getting that thing on the bus!"* I shouted over to them.

Soon the bus drew away and Paul and I were on our way home. It felt strange not having the burden of the tea chest bass to cope with - just John Lennon's guitar. Instead of waiting John and Pete decided to walk to the next bus stop, which was in the direction of Woolton Village.

- *"Hey John, I think we've got trouble!"* shouted Pete suddenly as he looked over his shoulder.

Sure enough, in the distance Rod and Willo were appearing fast.

- *"Quick, here's the bus let's make a run for it."* cried John.

They both ran as fast as they could while carrying the tea chest. Finally John gave up.

- *"Pete we're just going to have to drop it."*

With that they dropped the tea chest and only just managed to board the departing bus. The buses in those days had an open platform that had a vertical rail which even when the bus was in motion, could be grabbed hold of and you would eventually manage to clamber on board, being pulled along by the bus' momentum.

- *"Phew that was a close one!"* sighed John as they both climbed onto the top deck of the bus.

- *"It looks as though we've seen the last of the tea chest though."*

- *"Yeah, Len will be pleased. He's always moaning about it."*

- *"If it comes to it we can always make another one. Anyway I'd sooner that Rod and Willo kick the tea chest round than our heads. Got a fag?"*

They both began to relax - but not for long!

Rod and Willo had managed to board the bus at the next bus stop, having run after it as fast as they could.

It was therefore a great surprise to the two friends when Rod and Willo appeared on the top deck.

- *"Call yourself a singer,"* Rod snarled at Lennon, *"I've heard better sounds from a sewing machine."*

Pete and John took evasive action by putting their arms up over their faces and crouching down behind the seats while the bus arrived at the next stop. Although Pete was also on the receiving end of the blows it was John that they were really after.

John somehow managed to duck down and make a run for the stairs. They immediately followed and having made the assumption that he had alighted, quickly jumped off the bus as it was about to drive away. Pete Shotton recounted the outcome to me recently;

- *"I came down from the top deck expecting to see John and these thugs fighting it out on the pavement. To my surprise and delight I found that John had managed to "lose himself" on the lower deck of the bus, by sitting between two old ladies and acting as though nothing had happened."*

That poor old tea chest was subjected to a lot of battering by the elements as it lay discarded by the road side by John and Pete in their time of need. However, at the weekend Ivan Vaughan and myself having deep down a great affection for the "old thing". We managed to retrieve it and brought it back to Ivan's house, where we eventually restored it to it's former glory.

6

A Near Fatal Illness and the Emergence of "The Beatles":

Our last Quarrymen performance for the year 1957 was at Wilson Hall in Garston on the 7th of December.

During the latter part of 1957 John Lennon had enrolled at Art College and Pete Shotton at the Police Academy as a police cadet. Eric Griffiths obtained an engineering apprenticeship at Napiers Engineering and Colin Hanton was nearing the end of his time as a trainee upholsterer. Rod Davis entered the sixth form at Quarry Bank school while Paul McCartney, Ivan Vaughan and myself were about to take our trial examinations in December 1957 to find out what subjects we would be able to take the following June for our General Certificate of Education.

With John Lennon now at the Art College we were studying practically next door to one another and would meet up at lunchtime on a regular basis. I can remember John introducing us to his newly found friend, Stuart Sutcliffe.

By this time I had got to know Paul McCartney not only as a new member of the Quarrymen but as a personal friend as well. We would often meet up in morning assembly at school with the main intention of giving Paul a chance to try out his counterpoint harmonies to the hymns that were being sung. Thus, "Onward Christian Soldiers" developed into a type of Everly Brothers duet for us both.

We would often get the bus home together after school finished at 4 p.m. Sometimes we would get the No. 80 bus whose end destination was the Speke area of Liverpool which meant that Paul and I would alight at Penny Lane in order to change buses. Whilst on the No. 80 bus one evening I can remember Paul talking to a young lad who I later found out was George Harrison. George was about 18 months younger than us but as Paul explained to me, George was already a very good guitarist. Their conversations were therefore generally confined to discussing the Quarrymen's progress and guitar playing in general. On one occasion Paul persuaded John and the rest of the group to come and hear this "guitar virtuoso". We went round to George's house in Speke and were duly impressed with his expert rendition of instrumentals such as "Raunchy" and "Guitar Boogie". George must have been encouraged by our favourable reaction as he became an avid follower and admirer of John Lennon. Much to John's annoyance, as he regarded George as "only a young lad". He was therefore not to be taken as a serious contender for entry into the close knit circle and there certainly wasn't any mention of him entering the Quarrymen at that time.

Paul and I would often meet together during the autumn evenings of 1957. I would cycle up to Forthlin Road and then we would walk up Clevely Road which ran directly off Mather Avenue and led up to Allerton Golf Links. Associated to this golf course was a ladies tennis club and one of our regular activities would be to watch, admire and sometimes criticize the ladies' tennis playing. Although if the truth be told we were attracted more to the women's legs than their tennis playing. Paul did occasionally play with his brother Michael at a club in Garston so he was able to cast a more objective eye over the proceedings. Afterwards we would stroll back to Paul's house for an evening cup of cocoa.

I can remember arranging to meet Paul to go to the Gaumont Cinema in Allerton Road. Unfortunately my parents had decided on this occasion that I was not allowed to go as I had been going out a lot recently and was not spending enough time at home. There was no way of letting Paul know about the change of plan as we were not linked by telephone; Paul didn't have one and my father had decided to have ours taken out as it was hardly ever used. At about 6:30 p.m. there was a knock at the door. I knew immediately who it would be. I answered the door.

- *"What's up Len, why weren't you there? I waited until 5:45."* asked Paul.

- *"I'm sorry mate but I've got to stay in this evening and there was no way of letting you know. It's just one of those things."*

- *"Who's that at the door?"* my mother shouts from the kitchen.

- *"It's only Paul Mum, wanting to know why I didn't come out."*

This was a signal for Mum to come to the door.

- *"Hello Paul. I'm sorry you've had to come all this way but I'm afraid that Len has to stay in for a little while. He's been going out too much recently and his school work has been neglected as a result."*

- *"Oh, er, well, yeah I understand because sometimes my Dad says the same thing. Okay then Len, I'll see you around. Cheerio."* With that Paul walked back down towards Penny Lane where he was to catch his bus home.

1958 arrived and I reached the age of sixteen on the 6th of January. In the early part of 1958 the Quarrymen seemed to cram in a lot of engagements, mainly at Wilson Hall. Wilson Hall was handy for getting to and now that the threat of Teddy Boy gangs was receding our fear of it's tough reputation vanished. Bookings tailed off after January for which my parents were grateful as I was due to take the G.C.E. ordinary level examinations in the June of that year and more of my time could therefore be devoted to study.

I was also beginning to realize that the tea chest bass was looking out of place in the group especially as the skiffle boom had now ended and we were playing far more Rock 'n' Roll songs. These feelings turned out to be a sort of premonition as something rather serious happened to me in early August 1958.

I was sitting at home at 77 Lance Lane at the dining room table about to eat a banana (my favourite food). My father since told me that I just crushed the banana in my hand and suddenly fell on the floor unconscious. The ambulance was called and I was taken to Smithdown Road Hospital.

I can remember waking up a few days later, for I had been in a coma, and asking for a cigarette. Eventually I was transferred to Fazakerly Hospital which was situated about six miles away, to the north end of Liverpool.

I was diagnosed as suffering from Tubercular Meningitis. I was placed in an isolation cubicle and told that I was very fortunate to be alive with all my faculties intact, as this was a killer disease which sometimes left people mentally retarded, blind or with other impairments. This disease is contracted by breathing in infected droplets in unventilated, crowded conditions. I immediately thought then of all the times that I had spent with the Quarrymen in crowded, smoky atmospheres. I realized that I was lucky to be alive.

Obviously, while I was in hospital "the band played on" and the Quarrymen continued to perform and develop. It was soon after this time that George Harrison joined the group, so the line up now had; John Lennon, Paul McCartney and George Harrison on guitars. Colin Hanton was also still playing with them on drums. It took me quite a while before I realized that Nigel Whalley was also in the same hospital as me, although within a different section, he had been admitted for treatment for pleurisy (fluid on the lungs). I had a lot of visitors, the lads had not forgotten about me, they weren't that sort of people.

While I was in the isolation cubicle Lennon and McCartney, who had obviously formed a bond between themselves by then, came to visit me. They did not arrive at the ordinary visiting hours however, arriving on the ward at about 5 p.m. It was amazing that they had been allowed in. I suppose that if time had leaped ahead ten years then they would have been given the run of the place.

I remember one day when it was time for my temperature to be taken by the female duty nurse, and on hearing her footsteps down the corridor I told John and Paul to make a quick exit through the french doors that led out onto the garden area, I wasn't sure whether or not they had asked for permission to visit me, anyway, they did as I asked. Whilst the staff nurse (who was middle aged) was holding my wrist to take my temperature, I could see these heads appearing outside and faces being pulled, thumbs up signs etc. I found it difficult to keep a straight face and the nurse thought that I must be in pain. I quickly assured her that I was okay and when she left they came in again and filled me in on all the latest news.

The duration of my stay in hospital was from the August of 1958 up until the April of 1959, a total of some seven months in total.

I was later transferred to a double room which I shared with a young lad who was recovering from tuberculosis. While I was in this double room I had a visit from George Harrison, who came to visit me on his own and although I didn't know him all that well I really appreciated the visit because he seemed so understanding and caring.

Eventually I was transferred to the main hospital ward as I was now able to walk. I still had a crew cut and I remember another funny instance. The matron had a pet Robin which she brought round in a small cage and she had a habit of letting it out to fly around the ward. Perhaps she believed that it might be good therapy for us. One time this little bird decided to fly to it's imagined nest - right on top of my crew-cut head. She quickly shouted for a camera and took a photograph.

Once virtually the whole class came in to see me, including Duff Lowe who sometimes played the piano with the Quarrymen and Neil Aspinall, who was later to become a member of the Apple Corporation.

One Sunday afternoon I received a visit from John Lennon and Ivan Vaughan. We decided to visit the snooker hall that was situated within the grounds of the hospital near to my ward. Lennon as usual started to play the fool, pretending to do trick shots by potting the balls whilst sitting on the edge of the table and looking in the opposite direction - he hadn't changed at all. I appreciated these visits a lot, particularly as the lads had to travel such a long way by public transport. They would have had to get two buses to Fazakerley and once at the main gate it was about a mile walk to where my ward was situated. It was reassuring to know that I hadn't been forgotten and that they were truly good friends.

One day, it must have been in late 1958 or early 1959, Lennon and McCartney came to see me and informed me that they were thinking of changing the band's name to the "Silver Beatles". I couldn't understand at first how the word "beatles" was spelt because when I first heard the name I began to envisage crawling insects. Then it was explained to me that it was "Beatles" with an "a" and I thought that it was rather a clever name. They also informed me that they had been to a recording studio in Kensington and made a demo disc which consisted of "That'll be the day" on one side and their own composition of "In Spite of all the Danger" on the other. I was impressed, they seemed to be going places fast.

Meanwhile, I grew stronger and fitter, gradually progressing to full health and I was discharged from the hospital in the spring of 1959, at the age of 17. I can remember going back to 77 Lance Lane and immediately noticing how small the house looked, it was an obvious reaction to having been in hospital for so long.

I realised after my discharge from the hospital that my lifestyle had to change.

I could no longer visit the places I used to, with their smoky and unventilated atmospheres. From now on it was going to be good food, exercise and fresh air. However, I did not give up my love of music and singing. I then decided to renew my studying at the Institute which had been so neglected and I enrolled at part time day school and also night school in order to obtain more GCE passes.

I would still ride down to Paul's house in Forthlin Road and I can remember one Saturday afternoon when they were all there. George Harrison with his girlfriend (they disappeared upstairs), John Lennon with his new girlfriend Cynthia sitting on the couch in the front room, and Paul McCartney. I spent the afternoon getting to know the latest news and found out that they had acquired a permanent venue for the band. This was to be the Casbah in West Derby, owned by Mona Best, the wife of Johnny Best the boxing promoter. I went along one night to watch them and was surprised at the minute size of the stage area, but down in the basement of this large house. It was very similar to the Cavern Club - bare brick walls, low ceilings, brick arches, etc.

I can remember calling for Paul one early evening and he said he had arranged to meet Lennon as they were going to play at the Casbah that very evening. So we decided to walk through Allerton Golf Course together, with Paul carrying his guitar. We had just turned onto Menlove Avenue to walk towards John's

—Bus Stop. The corner of Yew Tree Road and Menlove Avenue where Paul would meet John.—

house when we both saw him walking along - he had come to meet Paul. It was at the bus stop on the corner by Calderstones Park. They invited me to go with them to the Casbah but I didn't feel part of the band anymore and declined their invitation on that day.

I decided then, after that moment, that I would go on my way and leave them to go on theirs and that I needed to concentrate in gaining more educational qualifications in order to build a career for myself (it sounds dull, doesn't it?). It wasn't really what I wanted, I would still have liked to have been involved with the band, but I was under some pressure from my parents and felt that I owed it to them for supporting me through my serious illness. I studied further therefore, and obtained more GCE qualifications.

I was eventually articled to a firm of architects in Liverpool at the age of 18 in 1960, studying for the main qualification part time at the Liverpool College of Building.

Meanwhile, the Beatles as they were then known, were making a name for themselves at the Cavern Club in Liverpool (the place where John Lennon got thrown off stage). I used to go and watch them play the Cavern lunchtime sessions - there would be long queues of teenagers down Matthew Street waiting to get in to see them. You could hear the music right down the street, the whole street seemed to reverberate with the beat. The office I worked in was just across the way from the Cavern.

Although I could have gone backstage to speak to them I didn't, because I felt outside the music circle at that time. I was on the usual career road which everybody else seemed to think they had to go down and it depressed me to an extent to see the lads still enjoying their music, and although it was in my blood I seemed trapped into a career.

There were two incidents when I happened to run into the lads again in the course of everyday life. I was down at the pier head with a friend one day when The Royal Iris, a ferry boat that did dance cruises along the Mersey, docked at the landing stage. Out stepped Lennon, McCartney, Harrison and Ringo. Lennon seemed pleased to see me and asked how my architectural career was progressing, then he introduced me to Ringo and the lads went on their way.

The second instant was when I bumped into Paul McCartney in Smithdown Road. It must have been in 1961, when I was 19. I had gone to buy a newspaper for my father on my trusty Raleigh Rudge when I heard someone running after me shouting my name. I turned around and saw Paul running towards me. He was wearing orange shoes, which I complemented him on, and he seemed quite excited (probably because he'd just seen me, ha,ha!). Anyway, he told me that they had just got an invitation to appear on Granada Television. I felt like saying; *"It's alright for you, you seem to be having great fun and making a name for yourself while enjoying what you're doing"*. However, as you do, you never really express your real thoughts and I politely wished him all the very best.

Throughout my working life, mainly within the architectural profession, I have maintained an interest in music and singing. I married a Liverpool girl named Susan in 1965 and with our two sons Robert and Jonathan, left Liverpool in 1971 and went to live in Somerset. It was in the little town of Chard, Somerset where I became involved in taking the part of a lead vocalist in a rock gospel musical called "Come Together". This initially had been organized and started in America by the singer Pat Boone. We toured the south west area of England and I had the pleasure of singing solos in places like Bath Abbey, a wonderful experience for me. Our daughters were born to us in the south west of England; the eldest Ruth in Taunton and our youngest daughter Jane in Exeter, Devon.

After having lived in Exeter for a number of years we emigrated to New Zealand in October 1987 with our two daughters but could not manage to settle and arrived back in England in late February 1988. My wife, myself and our two daughters finally settled again in Liverpool, where we still live to this day.

In 1992 I linked up with Duff Lowe and Rod Davis. Duff Lowe had appeared with the Quarrymen occasionally and Rod Davis, who was the banjo player when the Quarrymen were first formed. We got together to do some recording at the Amadeus Studios in Liverpool which was organized by a promoter from Manchester.

When we met at the studios, the promoter Tony Davison asked the question "Who's going to do the singing?", I told him that I was willing and the decision was therefore made that I would do most of the vocals.

Following this demo tape, which was done very quickly in virtually two days, the promoter was so thrilled at the outcome that he requested that we get back together to make a second set of recordings a few months later. After having made this first set of recordings I sent a letter to Paul McCartney, asking for his advice and help, stating that I had got some of the original Quarrymen back together. A few months went by and I forgot that I had even written the letter. However, one Sunday afternoon in February 1992, the telephone rang at about two o'clock in the afternoon. My daughter Ruth answered and said, *"Dad, Paul is on the phone"*. I said, *"I don't know anyone called Paul."* Nevertheless, I answered. I heard a voice saying, *"Hi Len, it's your old mate here, Paul! I bet you think this is a wind up!"*. It was a surprise to me that after over thirty years we could have quite a relaxed conversation. He talked about his family, I talked about mine. He talked about animals and his vegetarianism. I asked him if he put his children under any pressure to choose not to eat meat and also whether he was ever scared that his life might be in danger following what had happened to John. He replied that he was not in the least worried and that he was ready to meet the "big man in the sky" at any moment.

I eventually sent off a tape to Paul and received a reply stating that he was impressed by my vocals and that when we got it together a bit more he would be willing to pass the tape on to some important people. However, soon after this we had problems "getting it together" as an outfit and there was a clash of personalities. In the end nothing further was done.

I have, in recent years, attended a number of different Beatles conventions. At the Amsterdam convention in 1993 I appeared on national T.V. and radio, having been asked to sing part of the then unknown and unheard of song, "In Spite of All the Danger". However, because Duff Lowe, who owned the original recording, had sold it to Paul McCartney and had agreed not to publicly perform

—Rod Davis & Len Garry : Amsterdam 1993.—

the song, I felt obliged only to sing "part" of the song. This was performed with Rod Davis on the guitar.

I have also appeared at recent Beatles conventions in Liverpool as a guest singer, in particular with the Scott Wheeler band from Boston. Most recently, I have linked up with Chris Tassone, a promoter and Ringo Starr "look-alike" who I met at the 1995 Beatle convention.

Postscript -

Many people have asked me about my early days because I was a friend of John and Paul's. They tend to ask me questions like *"Was there any indication that these lads had the potential to become superstars?"* I would always reply, *"Of course not. We were just a bunch of lads having fun"*. Yet, when I think about it again I realize that even though the fun element was of major importance, especially considering the type of instruments that we were playing at the time, there was also a very serious side.

We tried our best to copy our favourite singers such as Elvis Presley, Chuck Berry and the like. The influence of Lonnie Donnegan was huge, as he gave such encouragement to thousands of young people to play their own music. However, the main influence on Lennon and the rest of us was when Elvis Presley came onto the scene. By that time we were already playing and John Lennon knew a few basic guitar chords. Of course it was primitive but then skiffle and even Rock 'n' Roll is fairly primitive. Without this essence of rawness in the music it would be lifeless and would not stir up any emotions. That was why the early blues and gospel songs that sprang from the southern American states moved people and touched their emotions so effectively. The gospel and blues were born out of suffering and they were trying to convey messages of real life and in this they were very effective. Skiffle and Rock 'n' Roll were born out of this type of music.

Without the Quarrymen there would have been no Beatles. Like everything in life that has been tremendously successful someone has to come up with the initial idea. In this particular instance it was John Lennon who had had the original idea of forming a musical band. He discussed this idea with Pete Shotton, who remained his friend throughout his life, Pete assured him that it was a good idea and encouraged him to go ahead. This was the "Birth of the Beatles", the embryonic beginnings of the world's most famous band, not the Cavern Club as is sometimes proposed. The Cavern Club in those early days usually threw us off.

People say to me, *"Len, just think, if you had stayed with the group you would be so rich now!"*. I always reply, *"Yes, but then I might also be dead"*. I don't believe that anything happens by chance in this life. I believe that it was planned that I should be there and form part of the Quarrymen in the early days and that my early friendship with John Lennon and Paul McCartney was also meant to be.

John Lennon was always something special. He was unique. During my teenager friendship with him he was always a lad that was full of fun and also someone with a marvellous gift for innovation and originality - starting new hairstyles, etc. etc. He never seemed to care much what people thought about him. He had a vicious contempt for anything that showed hypocrisy or established views that reeked of elitism. He was a true "Working Class Hero". Lennon would have made the headlines if he had had to make it on his own. To me he will always remain in my memory the leader of "the gang" that used to fool around on the grassy bank in the summertime. The leader of the Quarrymen who would always be the centre of attention if the gang ever went out anywhere.

I believe that it was right for me to have contracted tubercular meningitis when I was 16 years old, even though this in fact sealed my exit from the group and the end of my friendship with John Lennon and Paul McCartney. The only envy I ever felt for their fame and fortune had nothing to do with the fact that they had the adulation of the world, or with the fact that they were earning millions of pounds. It was the fact that they were earning money not only by doing the thing that they loved most but that in doing so they were also using their best talents. I have always felt a sense of frustration because I have always wanted to earn my living as a singer and to this day it is still the activity that I get the most pleasure out of. You see, I admire someone who keeps heading for their dream. People might try to knock them and say things about them but it's all to no avail. The Beatles in the early days in Hamburg went through some terrible ordeals, such as hunger and hardship. They must have felt like giving up often but to their credit they kept on going.

It was no chance that Paul McCartney met John Lennon that day at the St Peter's Church garden fête in 1957. It led to the combining of two unique talents which would form the best (in my opinion) song writing partnership ever known — a joining — a merging of two different personalties.

McCartney never had the cutting, sardonic humour of John Lennon, in fact as a personality I could never even see him fitting in with the Quarrymen, we were all linked by our common outlook on society and our very critical sense of humour. McCartney never seemed to share this in my opinion. Yet musically he was just what John Lennon needed. I can only liken the effect to the "Mona Lisa" without the smile - you add the smile and you have a master piece. So it was with John Lennon and Paul McCartney.

I have never regarded myself as anyone special and yet people sometimes say to me, *"Len, you have a unique place in musical history"*. However, when I think about this seriously then I start to realize that this is probably true because there is still a worldwide following of Beatles music. I am amazed that at many Beatles conventions there are so many young people who are avid followers, whereas you would expect the following to be in the age group of the middle 50's.

People are fascinated by John Lennon and Paul McCartney's songs yet their songs for me are quite often a wind up! The humour I used to know comes through in these songs as well as in their performances. For example;

Penny Lane -

This song was about *Penny Lane*. There *was* a *barber's shop* and the various people that lived and worked in this area would use the barber. There *was* a *bank* which actually was *on the corner*. It used to be called Martin's Bank and the bank or bank manager would probably be one of the few people who had a *motor car* in those days.

Penny Lane was the name given to the roundabout area that was also a bus terminus. It was a junction of five roads; Heathfield Road, Church Road, Smithdown Road, Penny Lane and Elm Hall Drive. The area by the roundabout on which the banker and the barber were was known as Smithdown place.

"Full of fish and finger pies in summer". As I stated previously there would be quite a number of teenagers "migrating" down to the Penny Lane area on a Saturday night during the summertime, wheeling their bikes with their girl friends on their arms, going to buy fish and chips from the shop. Lennon and the gang would saunter down there ourselves as it was regarded as a "family safe" area -not inhabited by any Teddy Boy gangs.

Penny Lane itself is a rather non-descript road that branches off Smithdown Place. It consists of a number of re-bricked terraced houses, some shops, a wine bar and St Barnabas' Church Hall (now Dovedale Towers). The Quarrymen played a gig there in 1957, when it was known as Dovedale Towers.

There was a bus shelter in those days as the roundabout was used as a bus terminus. I can remember there always being a newspaper salesman there and my Dad would often say to me, *"Len, get on your bike and get me a Football Echo"*, this was a special edition of the local paper that would come out on Saturday and gave the football results, it still happens now.

—Penny Lane bus shelter 'Roundabout'.—

I don't think that anyone at that time knew where Penny Lane was. I certainly didn't know at the time. I think it was generally assumed that "Penny Lane" was the small community around the roundabout and it was a very pleasant phrase that sounded good and slipped off the tongue very easily - rather better than "Smithdown Place". This is why it led to a song. *Penny Lane* and *Strawberry Fields* brought back memories to John Lennon and Paul McCartney of the times

—The Barber's shop Penny Lane - was Bioletti's - now Tony Slavin.—

that they had spent as teenagers, when life was carefree. It is a wonder that Lennon hadn't written a song about the days in Calderstones Park - a park that he loved so much, as I do to.

I was deeply shocked when I heard about John Lennon's tragic death. In fact it affected me so much that I had to take a few days off work. I was living and working in Exeter, Devon, at the time. John, because of his personality and lack of care about other people's opinions, became the target of a cult following unlike Paul McCartney who seemed to most people to be like "the boy next door". This type of cult following attracts those with obsessive tendencies, John was the unfortunate target of such a man as this.

I was tempted to contact John during his years of fame but I never did, although I believe that Pete Shotton kept in touch even though John had gone to live in America. I personally was satisfied with a happy married life and four lovely children. I just got on with everyday living. I felt that God had blessed me very much and I still hold the same opinion. This does not mean that I don't still have dreams, I do. My dream would be to one day give a concert in a large theatre with a full backing orchestra. Perhaps it will come true one day. Take note reader - hold on to your dreams!

7

Epilogue- The "Quarrymen" Now:

Rod Davies:

Rod Davies left the Quarrymen in the summer of 1957, deciding to concentrate more on his academic studies at Quarrybank and he moved up to the 6th form. He moved on from his banjo playing and learned how to play the guitar. He played in a jazz trio at Quarry Bank and his interest in folk music, which had always been there during his days with the Quarrymen grew.

In 1960 he went to study modern languages at Cambridge University and became interested in bluegrass music, learning to play the mandolin and the fiddle. After Cambridge he went to teach English in Regensburg, Germany, from 1963 to 1964, returning to his home in Liverpool soon after. Here he taught French and Spanish until 1968 when he became an expedition driver for Mini

Treck Expeditions at Kingston on Thames in Surrey. He would take the trips to Russia, Turkey and across the Sahara Desert.

In 1970 he married one of his ex-passengers and went to work for the YHA (Youth Hostel Association) organizing their adventure holiday programmes. He settled down in Hertfordshire and had two children, Sophie (now 22 years old) and Jonathan (now 20). He worked for a number of companies in the travel industry including Yugotours. He was divorced in 1982. In the early 1980's he played guitar for an American band and helped to revive the name of the Bluegrass Ramblers, playing at Britain's top bluegrass festival, supporting many big name American artists in the folk music field.

He became a "Tourism" lecturer in the late 1980's working at Uxbridge College. In 1996 he retired from lecturing and is now writing, publishing and translating .

Eric Griffiths:

His exit from the Quarrymen came soon after I had fallen ill in August 1958. He says that he left the Quarrymen because George Harrison had been asked by John to join the group at about this time. It was the period when electric guitars were being introduced and there would have been four guitar players had he stayed; George, Paul, John and himself. He was asked if he would consider buying himself a bass guitar but this would have meant that he would also have had to buy an amplifier. Two factors therefore contributed to his exit from the group; firstly, George Harrison was a better guitarist than Eric, and secondly, he could not afford to buy himself an amplifier.

The line up after Eric Griffiths left was; Paul McCartney, John Lennon, George Harrison and Colin Hanton, with John Lowe standing in on the piano. He left just before the new line up of the group made their first recording of "In Spite of All The Danger" and "That'll be The Day".

Eric had been on an engineering apprenticeship at Napiers Engineering in Liverpool at the time of his departure from the group but he left this apprenticeship six months after obtaining it and joined the Merchant Navy. He managed to obtain three passes at ordinary level in the General Certificate of Education. At sea he progressed from a Deck Officer Cadet to that of Third Mate and then Second Officer. At the age of 24 he married a Liverpool girl at St Peter's Church in Woolton (where the garden fête was held in 1957). He had a variety of jobs after he was married but eventually joined the Home Office as a work study officer for Her Majesty's Prison Service, which involved a good deal of travel visiting various state prisons all around the country. He moved to

Market Harborough in 1969.

He moved to Scotland with his wife and three children in 1972 and became Head of Planning and Production for the Prison Service. He now lives in Edinburgh, having left the prison service and opened a dry cleaning chain.

At the 40th anniversary of the Cavern's opening in February 1997 I became re-acquainted with Eric after 39 years. He is now getting involved in our Quarrymen charity performance on July 5th 1997 (the anniversary of when Paul met John) at St Peter's Church Hall. The event is being organised in order to raise money to repair the village hall. Almost all of the original members will be taking part; Pete Shotton, Eric Griffiths, Colin Hanton, Rod Davis and myself.

Colin Hanton:

Colin Hanton played for the last time with the Quarrymen at Finch Lane bus depot. This gig had been arranged for them by the father of George Harrison who was a bus driver himself. It was in January 1959.

According to Colin they had been asked to play two sessions and the manager from the Pavilion Theatre in Lodge Lane was in the audience to audition the Quarrymen for a spot in his theatre. The first session went down quite well with the audience but after this word got around that there were free pints of beer available for the group at the bar.

The whole of the group were therefore pretty drunk by the time it came to doing the second set. John and Paul who were "under the influence" began to take the piss out of George Harrison, which did not go down very well with George's parents who were sitting in the audience. Afterwards the manager of the Pavilion spoke to the group back stage and started to criticize their performance, saying that if they wanted a resident spot in his club then their behaviour and attitude would have to improve one hundred per cent. John did not take very kindly to being told what to do and told the manager to "Piss Off". According to Colin, on the bus home afterwards Pete Shotton and Colin had a row with Paul. After that fiasco Colin never continued with the group and apparently he was never asked to return.

Colin continued and finished his apprenticeship with the upholstery firm and now has his own upholstery business in Runcorn. He is married with two grown up daughters and lives in Liverpool. Colin was present at the 40th anniversary of the opening of the Cavern Club that was held recently and will also be taking part in the 40th anniversary charity show at St Peter's.

Pete Shotton:

After his graduation from the Police Academy in 1959 Pete Shotton became a fully fledged police constable. He was still in his late teens and he was placed on beat duty in one of the roughest areas in Liverpool. After nine months on night duty he decided to leave the police force.

He then went into partnership with the owner of the Old Dutch Café, on Smithdown Road in Liverpool. It became one of the few places that were open after midnight. John and Paul used to visit the place after a "gig" before catching the bus home from the Penny Lane roundabout which was about a ten minute walk from the café. By this time (around 1959), John and Paul were wearing black leather jackets and trousers and using the name "The Beatles". When John was asked where the name had derived from John told Pete that he and Stuart Sutcliffe were searching for a similar type of name to Buddy Holly's "Crickets". They came up with "Beetles" and John then had the idea of changing the "e" to an "a" to form a sort of pun on "beat" music. Whilst he was working nights at the Old Dutch Café Pete was able to join John and Paul for some of the lunch time sessions at the Cavern and so keep in constant touch with the group.

By December 1963 while Beatle mania was sweeping across Britain Pete received a phone call from John, asking him to meet him at Mimi's. When Pete arrived there John had just gone across to his Aunt Harriet's to collect some of his old books and take them back to Mimi's. Here John and Pete talked about the phenomenal success the Beatles were having and John asking Pete how the Old Dutch Café was getting on. In truth it wasn't doing very well but Pete didn't like to admit it openly to his friend. John, seeing that Pete was in for a miserable Christmas that year, handed him £50, which was John's weekly pay. Needless to say that Pete was very thankful for John's generosity. John then asked Pete what he wanted to do with his life. Pete told him that he would like to open a betting shop when he could afford it; John subsequently gave authority for Brian Epstein to write Pete a cheque out for £3,000. Pete by this time had been married to Beth and was living with Beth's mother, not very far away from the café.

Pete went round to Nems Enterprises to claim his cheque the next day. Brian was not in when Pete arrived that morning. While Pete was waiting for Brian to return the telephone rang and as there was no one in the office at the time Pete answered it. It happened to be Ed Sullivan's office wanting to speak to Brian. On Brian's return Pete informed him of the telephone call from Ed Sullivan (Pete not knowing who Ed Sullivan was). On hearing this Brian was jumping for joy at this news and explained to a bemused Pete Shotton the importance of the call. He was only too happy to issue Pete with the cheque and as Pete was leaving the office Brian asked him if he would like a job as his personal assistant. Although tempted, Pete liked the idea of being his own boss and now that he had the means to do so he decided to decline the offer. Furthermore Pete had been married for only nine months and didn't like the idea of spending a lot of time away from home.

The Beatles at Christmas time 1963 were playing at Finsbury Park's Astoria Theatre in London. Pete and Beth were invited to go down and stay at John Lennon's new flat in Kensington and watch them perform.

Pete and Beth accepted the invitation and were duly greeted by John's wife Cynthia and baby Julian. Pete left Beth with Cynthia and went to the show that evening and was overwhelmed by the reception given to the Liverpool lads. He met Nigel Whalley the Quarrymen's first manager who he hadn't seen for years. Backstage John greeted Pete and Nigel like long lost brothers and they had a mini Quarrymen re-union. Afterwards they went back to John's flat for a party.

Beth and Pete stayed at John's flat for the rest of the week, watching all the Beatles performances and going on sight-seeing tours with Cynthia and Julian. They had a memorable New Years Eve party with George and Ringo joining in the celebrations. Pete at this time, seeing all the fun that his old mate John Lennon was having and the money that he was making felt as though his life was dull and mundane in comparison. John, seeing Pete's state of mind reminded him that he now had the money to make a fresh start.

During the first few weeks of 1964 the Beatles virtually conquered America receiving rapturous applause and attracting huge crowds at every performance. In July of that year the Beatles had a home-coming reception for the Liverpool premier of "A Hard Day's Night" and also attended a civic reception held by the Lord Mayor of Liverpool. Pete Shotton was spectator in the crowd as the cavalcade of limousines went by the Old Dutch Café but Ringo spotted him and they all waved at him frantically.

John, while back in Liverpool still found the time to contact his old friend Pete and they arranged to meet up at Mimi's. The two had their usual discussion on how their mutual careers were proceeding with John asking Pete where the betting shop was; Pete explained to John about the obstacles he had found in obtaining a suitable property and that he had since spent the money.

John didn't seem perturbed at the news and insisted that Pete looked around for a really good business venture that would make him a lot of money. Pete was extremely grateful for John's continued generosity.

The Beatles embarked on their first tour of America and Pete began to look around for a suitable business venture. By the Christmas of 1964 John, George and Ringo had bought houses in the stockbroker belt of Surrey, whilst Paul decided to live in London. Pete decided to spend the Christmas holiday with his wife Beth down at Farnham on the south coast of England, staying with his sister Jean and husband Frank. Being bored one day he decided to go for a haircut. On leaving the barber's shop he spotted a business agency and decided to have a closer look to see what they had to offer. The agent showed Pete a sub Post Office combined with a supermarket situated on Hayling Island. After mentioning it to Frank they decided to take a look at the property the next day. Pete fell in love with the place right away as it was situated not very far from the beach. On returning to Liverpool Pete rang up John's accountants, telling them about the business and asking them to check it out for him. They soon reported back that the business was a sound proposition. By Easter 1965 Pete was the proud owner of a supermarket on an island which he had never even heard of just a few months earlier.

As far as Pete was concerned, one of the main assets of living on Hayling Island, which was situated off the Hampshire coast, was that it was only one hours drive away from John's residence in Weybridge. For the next few years Pete spent all his free weekends at "Kenwood" and in this way kept in close contact with John and the other three Beatles.

In the year 1965 the Beatles helped to bring London to the centre of the world fashion stage and it became the swinging capital of the sixties. It was a year within which the Beatles enjoyed and wallowed in their new found fame and fortune, frequenting the famous "night spots" in London where the rich and famous on the music scene spent their leisure time. Pete states that John meanwhile was gradually shying away from going out much in public and was on the verge of becoming a recluse.

In 1967 the Beatles were thinking of forming their own company the Apple Corporation and severing their ties with Brian Epstein. Pete meanwhile had settled down with his wife and son on Hayling Island and everything was going well for him when John contacted him and asked him to come to London in order to help run the new Apple Corporation. As far as John was concerned Pete had already agreed and before Pete could discuss the matter further John told everyone that Pete had accepted. Pete then tried to find out what his new role would be and found out that he was to run a boutique shop in London and that if this took off then more would open up around the country.

Pete was swept along by John and Paul's enthusiasm and within three weeks had arranged for his mother to take over the running of the supermarket. The arrangement was to be that Pete's wife and son would remain in their flat on Hayling Island and Pete would, after spending the weekdays running Apple, return to see them at the weekends. Pete spent the next year or so running the new company from their offices in Baker Street, London. However, he soon got disillusioned with the position and made the decision to leave, whereupon John offered him an alternative job as his personal assistant which Pete accepted. This involved paying his bills and chauffeuring him around but most of all it involved being his permanent companion and confidante.

After John Lennon met Yoko Ono Pete felt that John no longer needed him as a companion and he therefore decided to go back to working for himself. John had meanwhile bought a new home in Ascot called Tittenurst Park.

John and Yoko moved to New York in 1971 and Pete went into various new business ventures having decided to sell his supermarket. In the summer of 1976 Pete Shotton and his friend Paul Hepworth went on a tour of the U.S.A., taking in twenty nine states in the space of a few weeks. In late October Pete and Paul dropped in on Pete's brother Ernest and his wife June who lived in New Jersey, about fifteen miles from New York. A few days before Pete's return to the U.K. the pair spent a day in New York and found themselves walking in Central Park. Paul realised that they were not far from where John Lennon lived in the Dakota building. With a little persuasion from Paul the two agreed to call in on John. However, all they were allowed to do was to leave Pete's brother's name and telephone number. An hour later Pete had arrived back at his brother's house and he received a telephone call from John asking him to come over right away.

Pete found John to be looking a lot slimmer than when he had last seen him and by this time John and Yoko had baby Sean. John had arranged for the three of them to be driven to his favourite Japanese restaurant. Over the meal Pete and John chatted just like the old days when they would get together at Mimi's place. John had given up smoking and alcohol and apparently was now living on a diet of raw fish and brown rice. John asked Pete to give him a ring before flying back to England and he did this the next morning, but he felt as though the conversation was a little strained. Pete was given the strong impression that Yoko Ono did not like having him around, however, he said his farewells to the pair and tried to end on a friendly note with Yoko. John told Pete to give his love to England.

Pete Shotton never saw John Lennon again.

In 1995 I happened to see an article in the Liverpool Echo stating that a new restaurant had been opened recently in Liverpool called "Fatty Arbuckles" and that Pete Shotton was the owner.

On reading this I telephoned the manager and asked if he could contact Pete and give him my home telephone number. A day later I received a call from Pete and we arranged to meet at his restaurant in Edge Lane, Liverpool. On meeting Pete after thirty six years it was as though we had only been separated for a few weeks. We found that our friendship had stood the test of time despite having lost touch with one another.

We now see each other on a fairly regular basis as his head office is in Manchester. Pete will be appearing with the rest of the original Quarrymen at the 40th anniversary celebration of when John met Paul at St Peter's Church on the 5th of July 1997.

The only person missing will be John Lennon.

— Sue Garry - Chris Tassone - Len Garry. —

— Len Garry, Lisa & Gene Quondamatteo —

— Len Garry - Eric Griffiths - Pete Shotton —

— l to r Colin Hanton - Pete Shotton -Martin Lewis - Len Garry - Eric Griffiths - Rod Davis —

— Sue Garry - Len Garry - Burlington Ontario 1997 —

— Ruth Garry & Peter Bennett - Toronto 1996 —

— Ruth & Jane Garry - Beatle Convention 1996 —

— Rod Davis - Eric Griffiths - Len Garry - Pete Shotton - Colin Hanton - 'Duff' Lowe —

— Len Garry & Ernest, owner of "Mendips" for 35 years —

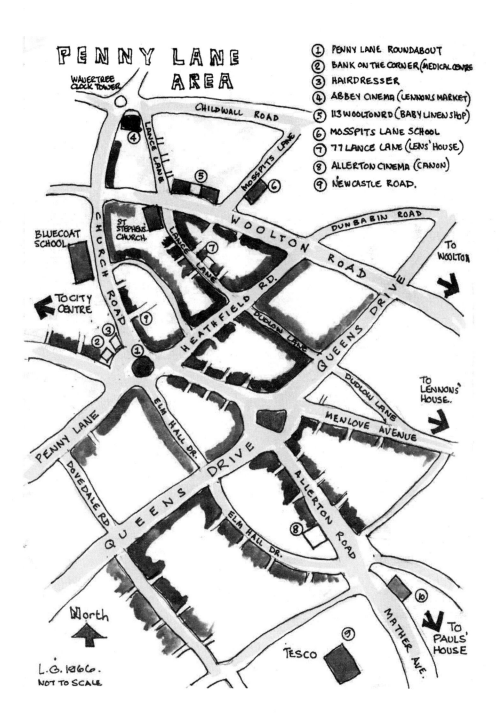

PENNY LANE AREA

① PENNY LANE ROUNDABOUT
② BANK ON THE CORNER (MEDICAL CENTRE)
③ HAIRDRESSER
④ ABBEY CINEMA (LENNONS MARKET)
⑤ 113 WOOLTON RD (BABY LINEN SHOP)
⑥ MOSSPITS LANE SCHOOL
⑦ 77 LANCE LANE (LENS' HOUSE)
⑧ ALLERTON CINEMA (CANON)
⑨ NEWCASTLE ROAD.

WAVERTREE CLOCK TOWER
CHILDWALL ROAD
LANCE LANE
MOSSPITS LANE
WOOLTON ROAD
DUNBABIN ROAD
BLUECOAT SCHOOL
ST STEPHENS CHURCH
CHURCH ROAD
LANCE LANE
TO WOOLTON
TO CITY CENTRE
HEATHFIELD RD.
DUDLOW LANE
QUEENS DRIVE
TO LENNONS' HOUSE.
DUDLOW LANE
MENLOVE AVENUE
PENNY LANE
ELM HALL DR.
QUEENS DRIVE
DOVEDALE RD.
ALLERTON ROAD
ELM HALL DR.
QUEENS DRIVE
North
L.G. 1866.
NOT TO SCALE
TESCO
MATHER AVE.
TO PAULS' HOUSE

CALDERSTONES PARK

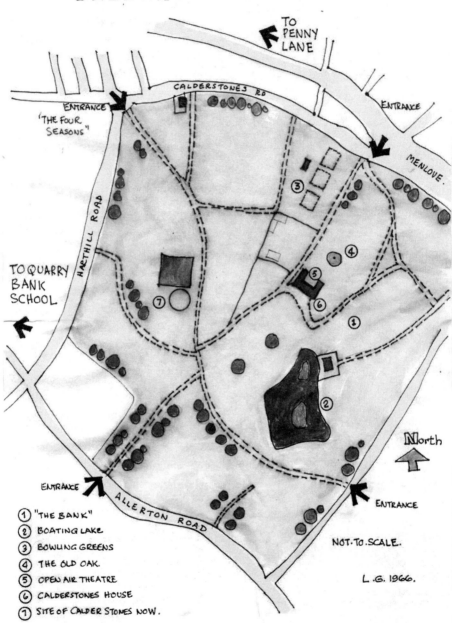

TO PENNY LANE

CALDERSTONES RD

ENTRANCE
'THE FOUR SEASONS'

ENTRANCE

MENLOVE.

HARTHILL ROAD

TO QUARRY BANK SCHOOL

③

④

⑤

⑥

①

⑦

②

North

ENTRANCE

ALLERTON ROAD

ENTRANCE

① "THE BANK"
② BOATING LAKE
③ BOWLING GREENS
④ THE OLD OAK.
⑤ OPEN AIR THEATRE
⑥ CALDERSTONES HOUSE
⑦ SITE OF CALDER STONES NOW.

NOT·TO·SCALE.

L.G. 1966.

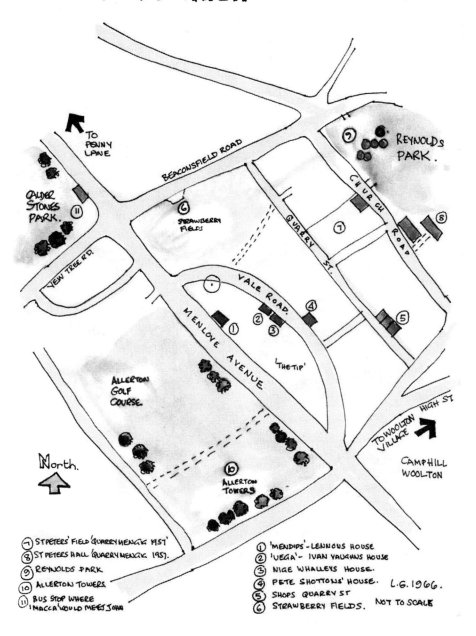

"MENDIPS" AREA

TO PENNY LANE

BEACONSFIELD ROAD

REYNOLDS PARK.

CALDER STONES PARK.

⑪

YEW TREE RD.

⑥ STRAWBERRY FIELDS

QUARRY ST.

CHURCH ROAD

⑦

⑦

⑧

VALE ROAD.

②③ ④ ⑤
①

MENLOVE AVENUE.

'THE TIP'

ALLERTON GOLF COURSE.

TO WOOLTON VILLAGE   HIGH ST

CAMPHILL WOOLTON

North.

⑩ ALLERTON TOWERS

⑦ ST PETERS' FIELD 'QUARRY MENGK 1957'
⑧ ST PETERS HALL 'QUARRY MENGK 1957'.
⑨ REYNOLDS PARK
⑩ ALLERTON TOWERS
⑪ BUS STOP WHERE 'MACCA' WOULD MEET JOHN

① 'MENDIPS'- LENNONS HOUSE
② 'VEGA'- IVAN VAUGHNS HOUSE
③ NIGE WHALLEYS HOUSE.
④ PETE SHOTTONS' HOUSE.   L·G·1966.
⑤ SHOPS QUARRY ST
⑥ STRAWBERRY FIELDS.   NOT TO SCALE

BUCKINGHAM PALACE

Martin Lewis, Esq

I send my sincere thanks to all those assembled at St. Peter's Church in Woolton, Liverpool, for their kind message of loyal greetings sent on the occasion of the celebration to mark the Fortieth Anniversary of the first meeting between John Lennon and Paul McCartney which led to the formation of the Beatles.

I received this message with much pleasure and send my best wishes to all concerned for a most enjoyable and successful occasion.

ELIZABETH R.

5th July, 1997.

10 DOWNING STREET
LONDON SW1A 2AA

THE PRIME MINISTER

I am delighted to send my best wishes to St Peter's Church in Woolton for your Garden Fete today. The Church will always hold a special place in the hearts of Beatles' fans the world over as the first place that John Lennon and Paul McCartney met 40 years ago. I am sure the comeback of the Quarry Men after all these years will prove a tremendous draw. I hope the sun shines and you have a wonderful day.

Tony Blair

July 1997

29.4.97.

Dear Jean and fellow organisers of :-

"The Fortieth anniversary of John Lennon meeting Paul McCartney."

In response to your very kind invitation I am afraid I am going to have to disappoint you all on this occassion.

I have the most wonderful memories of those precious days in Woolton. They hold a very special place in my heart.

The whole concept of your proposed celebration is wonderful and although due to other commitments I will be unable to attend.

I will most definitely be with you all in Spirit!

Please give all concerned my love and sincere best wishes for every success. for such a great cause!

Once again may I convey to you all how sorry I am not to be with you on This occassion

all my love
to you Jean and all the faithful
Fans.
X   Cynthia (Lennon).

A MESSAGE TO WOOLTON FROM PAUL McCARTNEY

Ah yes, I remember it well.

I do, actually. My memory of meeting John for the first time is very clear. My mate Ivan Vaughan took me along to Woolton here and there were The Quarry Men, playing on a little platform.

I can still see John now - checked shirt, slightly curly hair, singing *Come Go With Me* by The Del Vikings. He didn't know all the words, so he was putting in stuff about penitentiaries - and making a good job of it.

I remember thinking 'He looks good - I wouldn't mind being in a group with him'.

A bit later we met up; I played him *Twenty Flight Rock* and he seemed pretty impressed - maybe because I *did* know the words.

Then, as you all know, he asked me to join the group, and so we began our trip together. We wrote our first songs together, we grew up together and we lived our lives together.

And when we'd do it together, something special would happen. There'd be that little magic spark.

I still remember his beery old breath when I met him here that day. But I soon came to love that beery old breath. And I loved John. I always was and still am a great fan of John's. We had a lot of fun together and I treasure all those beautiful memories.

So I send you all in Woolton and Liddipool my best wishes today.

And thanks for remembering - there's no way that when we met here we had any idea of what we'd be starting. But I'm very proud of what we did. And I'm very glad that I did it with John.

I hope you all have a wonderful day and God bless all who sail in you.

PAUL McCARTNEY

What a sweet celebration!

Yes, the meeting of John and Paul was an important event not only for those of us who loved their songs, but for the whole world which went through a social change for the better as a result of their words and music.

John's first thought as Paul showed what he could do was: "Okay - this guy is good and already the girls are flocking around *him* - not around me! So if I let him in, he's going to be a tough one to handle - but I'll have a strong band."

So John took Paul in. I think this story is important in that it shows as a creator and a leader of the band, John went for getting a strong band rather than having an easy time. And John was only a teenager. What a brain! What a guy!

By the way, it's interesting that the meeting took place at a church. Also, the main bulk of their songs were recorded in *Abbey* Road Studios, in London. Am I the only one who thinks of these coincidences as interesting?

John and Paul were traveling minstrels, who spread the word of love throughout the world. Through their songs, they brought the energy of love to the then gray world, which was still coping with the aftermath of the second world war.

With their words and music, John and Paul showed the world that law and order was not necessarily the most important force in the world. Love was the power and the energy that could change the world. And it did.

But it all started at the Woolton Fete forty years ago. As you celebrate this day, the world joins you in your celebration. Those who cannot come physically to Liverpool join you in spirit. It's a nice day to celebrate and I thank you for doing it. Peace.

YOKO ONO

Mosspits Lane School Leaving Register E. 3000—416	NAME	II. Standard	III. Date of Birth	IV. REASON FOR PROPOSED REMOVAL OF NAME (If on account of non-attendance or Irregularity, columns V. and VI. must ALSO be filled up).
		Cl.		Sch.
Haas Margaret		V	6.12.40	Left district. Liddadale Rd
Ellison Joy		IV.	2.12.40 17.9.40	" " Wootton Sch
Davison Margaret		IV	12.9.40	Distance – Ill health
Hampson Patricia		IV	3.7.41	Left district – London.
Williams Janet		III	25.10.39	Left district:
Murray Douglas		III	4.9.39	Left district New Dothys employment ?
McGovern Barbara		II.	17.1.39.	Webelth Rd Lufts.
Price Gillian Mary		I	15.11.38	Dovedale Rd Lufts.
Till George Bernard		IV	14.9.40	Left district Surrey
Shieldhouse Ruth.		I	7.3.38	Rudston Rd.
Kirk John		IV	6.8.40	T.B. Spring – Heswall Hosp.
Lennon John		IV	9.12.40	Left District
Ebbs Patricia Ann		I	4.6.58	Mosspits Lane Juniors
Nicholson Robt. Bruce		I	28.8.38	" " "
Hendry Stuart Geddis		IV	23.4.40	Rudston Rd. Infts.
Moulton Ruth		III	27.4.40	Ill health – medical cert.
Hankey Edward		II	7.7.40	Left district – Widnes.
Wheeler Virien Christine		II	22.6.40	" " London.

— Mosspits Lane "Leaving register" - note Lennon's birthday is wrong —

The Summer of '55

Suburban trees and silly games
Were the order of the day and Pete
Shotton smoked his 'Passing Clouds' to
Pass the time away

Chorus   Days were long, summers strong in
The summer of fifty five
People change and move along to
An open world outside

Foolin' around on the hill
Sortin' out who's strong
Until we spied the 'Parky' man
Who moved us all along

chorus

Tubby Turner, freckles all, would
Roll up rather late and
Tell us all of funny tales of things
We loved to hate

chorus

Lennon dreamt of stardom
Ivy Vaughan would wave his hands
Len Garry took off 'Ernie Ford' and
Wore shoes with rubber bands

chorus

Little did we all know
Of things that were meant to be
Of fame fortune and Penny Lane
For all the world to see

Len Garry July 6th 1997

— Eric Griffiths - Len Garry - Pete Shotton - Rod Davis Live at St. Peter's hall on July 6th 1997—

— Colin Hanton - Rod Davis - Pete Shotton - Len Garry - Eric Griffiths - Live on the back of the flat-bed truck once again, July 6th 1997—

Bonus Interview CD
Len Garry and Pete Shotton Tour Liverpool and "Mendips"

—— 1.
Pete and Len talk to Ernest - owner of "Mendips".
—— 2.
Ernest - Mimi and "Mendips"- Lennon the "toughy" - Pete - "The Old Apple Tree" - Ernest - Uncle George
—— 3.
Ernest - buying "Mendips"
—— 4.
Lennon Mowing the lawn - The Tin Can Phone - "The Co-op Shuttle"
—— 5.
Lennon, McCartney & Harrison the "passing-out" parade - Quarrymen rehearsal venues.
—— 6.
"Mendips" - The 1963 parade - Lennon talks all night - Please Please Me
—— 7.
John's Bedroom - The dinner ticket scam - John's mail-order guitar
Julia Lennon's death
—— 8.
Shotton asks McCartney to join "The group" - Lennon's sidekicks
"Sibling" rivalry
—— 9.
Barbara Baker - Pranks and the bonfire incident
—— 10.
The tree - Nige Whalley
—— 11.
Ivan Vaughan - Strawberry Fields
—— 12.
St. Peter's Church - Lennon drunk?
—— 13.
St. Peter's Village Hall and The Quarrymen's gig - McCartney teachs Lennon chords
—— 14.
Lennon choirboy - Woolton Cinema - Rhind's photograph - "The Bellboy" - Lennon vanishes.